R O M A N
ITINERARIES

Text by Ettore Della Riccia
Introduction by Ceccarius

ENTE PROVINCIALE PER IL TURISMO
DI ROMA

Drawings by Enrico Montalto di Fragnito
Photos : C. D. D'Isola - A Drago
Maps by : V. Clementi

A MONG THE MANY ACTIVITIES *of the Ente Provinciale per il Turismo of Rome, that of the publication of information stands out. Noteworthy are the publications of texts suited to tourists of high cultural level, as well as to those with more superficial knowledge the high typographical standard of the texts and the choice and clarity of the illustrations. To achieve this end, the competent authorities of the Ente Provinciale per il Turismo of Rome carries out a careful sifting as to the choice of authors, who, as we have said, must be able to render their work comprehensible to readers of varying cultural levels, must know their subjects thoroughly and be able to sort the indispensable from the unnecessary, to put the reader into the correct historial picture, to render clear the majesty of the major monuments, and to interpret curiosities of an anecdotal nature. We repeat, all this is not easy, for writing about Rome is of such fascination and so rich in multiform events, that one would wish to recount everything, to illustrate all. Of course, the limitations imposed by the popular nature of the publications cause lacunae and abridgements which, if they escape the attention of the unlearned reader, may give a negative impression and bring severe criticism from those who consider that they know much or all of things Roman.*

Rome is indeed a difficult subject, not to be taken lightly even where a summary is intended. The bibliography of descriptions of the Eternal City considers thousands of texts in all languages. The universal character of the city justifies the interest which prompts

Editors to publish so-called «Guides» all over the world. The origin of these may be found in the texts of the ancient historians, in the rudimentary and naive annotations of mediaeval times, whence derives the picturesque listing of things marvellous, the «Mirabilia» in which fable and legend are interwoven with the historical sources. They follow on the descriptions of wanderings over the Seven Hills by Italians and foreigners who, in the course of time, followed the specific descriptions of antiquities, of sacred and profane monuments, of everything it is considered essential to see. After the seventeenth century texts, still illustrated with rudimentary woodcuts, came those of the eighteenth, adorned with clear engravings and brought up to date by the multiple editions of the nineteenth century, which gradually reached a high standard of perfection (it is enough to think of the various Touring Club guides), in texts worthy of consideration and which even today serve as basis for not a few foreign «guides». To quote authors and publishers would take too long. In any case, there is a sufficiency of up-to-date bibliographies to help the student, or even the tourist, of abundant material. In these, consultation is facilitated by indications, notes and a rational index.

Naturally, the Ente Provinciale per il Turismo of Rome, as in other of its publications, (e. g., the much-appreciated «Tourist pathways through the Province of Rome» by Bruno Palma) has wished to meet the desire for anecdotal curiosities on the part of the tourist whom we may define as «common», with little time at his disposal, but who wishes, just the same to see the principal things, to get a rough idea of the City's transformation, of its historical endurance through victories and defeats, triumphs and destructions, from Paganism to Christianity, from the temples of the «false, lying gods» to the triumph of the Faith of

6

Christ as affirmed by the splendid series of basilicas and churches. And all this without neglecting the town-planning developments, the vastness of the Vatican, the rise of suburbs which are true satellite towns for their size and population, the use of the most modern means of transport, the modernity of the sports accomodation, the vastness of the airports, the sea of Ostia only a few miles from the city centre ...

This is the arduous task given by the Ente Provinciale per il Turismo of Rome to one of the most famous journalists of the « Roman School ». I like to call him a « Reporter» giving to this too common expression is real meaning of annotator of and commentator upon civic events in their various aspects, among which we should pick out for particular mention, administrative and town-planning discussions, historical reviews, notes of local colour ... a diarist, in fact. Such is the author of this little work; Ettore della Riccia, not Roman by birth, but equally civitate donatus *for the many years he has lived there and for the Roman enthusiasm which fascinates, inspires, and guides him. Highly qualified as he is in Roman journalism, and for the other reasons already stated, he may consider himself suitable to « presenting » Rome in a rapid excursus to the thousands and thousands of visitors who will flood into the city for the Olympics, or for those who will make the ordinary tourist stay.*

In the fine edition brought out by the Ente Provinciale per il Turismo of Rome, this « Little Guide » can accompany, usefully and pleasantly, the tourist in his Roman hours or days, helping him to consider Rome, as ever and for ever, communis patria.

CECCARIUS

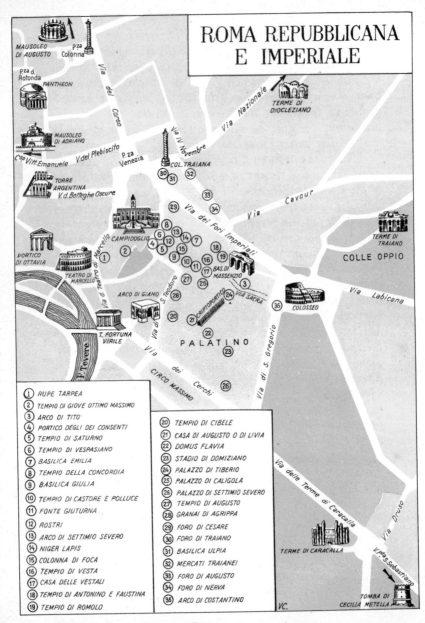

ROMA REPUBBLICANA E IMPERIALE

MAUSOLEO DI AUGUSTO · P.za Colonna

P.za d. Rotonda · PANTHEON

MAUSOLEO DI ADRIANO

Cso Vitt. Emanuele · V. del Plebiscito · P.za Venezia

Via del Corso

Via IV Novembre · COL. TRAIANA

Via Nazionale · TERME DI DIOCLEZIANO

TORRE ARGENTINA · V. d. Botteghe Oscure

CAMPIDOGLIO

Via dei Fori Imperiali

Via Cavour

TERME DI TRAIANO

COLLE OPPIO

PORTICO DI OTTAVIA

TEATRO DI MARCELLO

Via d. Teatro di Marcello

ARCO DI GIANO

Via di S. Teodoro

BAS. DI MASSENZIO

VIA SACRA

Via Labicana

COLOSSEO

T. FORTUNA VIRILE

CRIPTOPORTICO

PALATINO

Via di S. Gregorio

F. Tevere

CIRCO MASSIMO · Via dei Cerchi

Via delle Terme di Caracalla

TERME DI CARACALLA

V. Druso

V. P. S. Sebastiano

TOMBA DI CECILIA METELLA

VC.

① RUPE TARPEA
② TEMPIO DI GIOVE OTTIMO MASSIMO
③ ARCO DI TITO
④ PORTICO DEGLI DEI CONSENTI
⑤ TEMPIO DI SATURNO
⑥ TEMPIO DI VESPASIANO
⑦ BASILICA EMILIA
⑧ TEMPIO DELLA CONCORDIA
⑨ BASILICA GIULIA
⑩ TEMPIO DI CASTORE E POLLUCE
⑪ FONTE GIUTURNA
⑫ ROSTRI
⑬ ARCO DI SETTIMIO SEVERO
⑭ NIGER LAPIS
⑮ COLONNA DI FOCA
⑯ TEMPIO DI VESTA
⑰ CASA DELLE VESTALI
⑱ TEMPIO DI ANTONINO E FAUSTINA
⑲ TEMPIO DI ROMOLO

⑳ TEMPIO DI CIBELE
㉑ CASA DI AUGUSTO O DI LIVIA
㉒ DOMUS FLAVIA
㉓ STADIO DI DOMIZIANO
㉔ PALAZZO DI TIBERIO
㉕ PALAZZO DI CALIGOLA
㉖ PALAZZO DI SETTIMIO SEVERO
㉗ TEMPIO DI AUGUSTO
㉘ GRANAI DI AGRIPPA
㉙ FORO DI CESARE
㉚ FORO DI TRAIANO
㉛ BASILICA ULPIA
㉜ MERCATI TRAIANEI
㉝ FORO DI AUGUSTO
㉞ FORO DI NERVA
㉟ ARCO DI COSTANTINO

REPUBLICAN AND IMPERIAL ROME

CHAPTER I

REPUBLICAN AND IMPERIAL ROME

I N THE FAMOUS PHRASE attributed to Augustus, « I found a Rome of brick and left it of marble », is epitomized the essential difference between Republican and Imperial Rome. Two cities of which the second is a continuation of the first and whose architecture (a majestic architecture which still astonishes the world for its beauty and the refinement of its technique) represents the most direct witness of the continuity of a civilization thousands of years old.

Roman art grew out of Etruscan Italic and thence developed in direct contact with Greek; the former, rough and mainly technical, the latter refined. From the fusion of these two different concepts, that stylistic unity which became worldwide with the Roman Empire, was reached. If one considers Greek art, for example, one notes a fundamental difference existing between it and the art of Imperial Rome; while Greek art tended to an ideal of beauty, that of Rome is moved by a practical and realistic sense. Therefore, the works of major importance at Rome are not the temples, but the buildings which served the daily lives of the citizens : the baths, palaces, basilicas, acqueducts and theatres. We may say the same for sculpture, which was aimed above all at illustrating effectively the victorious deeds of the emperors and the Roman army.

The monuments which, after the centuries, we may still admire in the heart of the modern city, are a living witness of the two different periods. Of the Republican which, over five centuries, extended its domination over Italy, affirmed its power in the Mediterranean in the face of Carthage and Athens, pushed into Asia Minor and, under Julius Caesar, conquered Western Europe; and of the Imperial period, dominated by the figure of Augustus, who imposed himself as a « pacifier of peoples », fusing the East, the West and Africa into a just peace, and changing the face and spirit of Rome.

During the Republic the first great lines of communication were created, the first acqueducts were built, the early solemn temples rose and in the *Tabularium* (which we might call State Records Office) were enacted certain rigid principles of state administration. During the Empire, the Forum of Augustus was opened, the Imperial Palace was built on the Palatine (on the hill where the « square Rome » of Romulus was born), and there rose the Theatre of Marcellus, the Pantheon, the first baths open to the general public, the Colosseum, an architectural masterpiece, Trajan's Forum, the Baths of Diocletian, the Baths of Caracalla, the Basilica of Maxentius, the great imperial mausoleums, such as those of Augustus and Hadrian.

This rapid review gives a clear idea of the vastness of the material, which it is very difficult to study deeply in the sphere of a necessarily brief itinerary. We shall therefore consider only the principal zones, and shall begin our trip from the Capitol, that hill to which the " square Rome " of Romulus spread from the Palatine, extending over the intervening valley beneath, which was drained and chosen as a common market centre, becoming the Roman Forum.

The Capitoline Hill originally had another name, the *Saxum Tarpeium* or *Rupes Tarpeia*, the Tarpeian Rock, the terrible rock destined for the punishment of traitors (can be seen from the Palazzo della Consolazione). It is linked to the legend of the Roman girl, Tarpeia, who showed the Sabines, then at war with the Romans, a secret way on to the rock.

Statue of M. Aurelius in Piazza Campidoglio

The beautiful, but treacherous girl was hurled from the top of that height and the place, declared accursed, was chosen for the execution of tratiors of the fatherland and those who aspired to tyranny. According to another legend, Tarpea was buried on the rock itself, covered in the gold and jewels she had from the Sabines as a price for her betrayal.

The principal monuments of the Capitoline Hill, among which was the temple of Jove Optimus Maximus, faced the opposite way from today, having the front towards the Roman Forum, to which the hill was connected by the Via Sacra, the street for triumphal processions. The most important monuments of ancient Rome are gathered in the Roman Forum because it was here that the economic and political life of the city was centred. The greatest tribunes and orators spoke here; here paraded victorious captains and legions, it was the area given over to commerce, election meetings, administration of justice, election of magistrates, consuls, senators and of the supreme religious head, the Pontifex Maximus.

From the *Tabularium* — the building designed to hold the laws of the Roman State (*tabulae*) which is today united to the Palace — to the Arch of Titus, opposite the Colosseum, there is an innumerable succession of buildings, temples, votive and triumphal monuments, whose remains give an impression of solemn grandeur. Here are the ruins of the Portico of the Consenting Gods (of the major divinities of the celestial " consensus ") which, as one may read in the inscription on the architrave, was restored in the second half of the fourth century AD, by the city Prefect, Veius Agorius Praetextatus, one of the most ardent defenders of the dying paganism. Here are the ruins of the temples of Saturn, of Vespasian and of the Concordia : this last was founded by Furius Camillus in A. D. 367, to celebrate the concord established between patricians and plebs, after long struggles. Here, too is the Basilica Julia (to which corresponds, on the opposite side of the Forum, the Basilica Emilia) once one of the greatest buildings of the zone. It was begun by Julius Caesar, in the site of the ancient Sempronian Basilica, and completed by Augustus who, when it had been destroyed by fire, rebuilt it, enlarging it and calling it after his two young nephews and adopted sons, Gaius and Lucius Caesar. Here the tribunal known as the Centumvirs, to whom were entrusted civil cases, particularly those of inheritance, held their meetings. Having passed the Julian Basilica, one sees the temple of the Castori, of which three splendid Corinthian columns remain. It dates from the difficult period when Rome was passing from kingdom to republic. According to the legend, the Romans built this temple in fulfilment of the vow made to the Dioscuri (Castor and Pollux), who came to their aid in the battle against the Latin League at Lake Regillus. On that occasion the two young gods are said to have been seen watering their horses at a fountain, that of Juthurna, a pretty, square basin rising in the vicinity, dedicated to the nymph Juthurna, protectress of water. In the room round the tank, an altar with reliefs representing the Dioscuri, Leda and Helen dressed as the goddess of light, can be seen.

On the opposite side, near the Emilian Basilica, which we have already mentioned, are the rostrums, that is, the platforms from which the orators addressed the people. The name derives from the beaks (*rostra*) of ships taken in the battle against the people of Antium in 338 B.C., which decorated the front. The rostrum, which served mainly for parade speeches and official addresses during the Empire, consisted of a vast platform, several yards above the level of the square. On one side is the *umbilicus Urbis Romae*, a small, conical brick building, faced with marble, which was imagined to be the centre of Rome and of the Empire, and on the other, the *miliarium aureum*, a great marble column on which were inscribed the distances from Rome to the chief cities of the Empire.

There follows the Arch of Septimus Severus, in a very good state of preservation, because during the Middle Ages

TEMPLE KNOWN AS VESTA AND FORTUNA VIRILE

it was incorporated into other buildings of the period. It has three arches and is one of the largest triumphal arches in existence. It was dedicated in 203 A. D., to the memory of the Emperor to celebrate the victorious conclusion of his eastern campaign. Immediately at hand is the *Lapis Niger* and the column of Foca. The *Lapis Niger* is a small square area paved in black marble, under which tradition has it that Romulus' tomb lies, or the tomb of Faustulus, the shepherd who took him in. In fact, the remains of a kiosk which might well have been a tomb, have been found under the marble paving. The column of Foca, 46 feet high, was erected in A. D. 608, in honour of the Byzantine emperor of that name; it was crowned, as the inscription tells us, by the golden statue of the Emperor.

Still continuing towards the Palatine, we find the temple of the Divine Julius, erected by Augustus for the cult of Julius Caesar on the site where his body (he was killed in Pompey's Curia in the Campus Martius) was burned. The circular altar of tuff, enclosed by a niche, shows the exact point where the pyre was lighted. Not far away is the temple of Vesta which, with the nearby house of the Vestal Virgins, forms the most important part of the Forum from the religious point of view. Vesta, in fact, presided over the hearth and protected the fire which represented the perpetuity of the State. It was the duty of the virgin devoted to her cult to keep this fire always burning and to renew it each year on the first of March, the ancient New Year's Day of the Roman calendar, by rubbing a piece of wood on a board cut from a fruit-bearing tree.

Then we have the Temple of Antonius and Faustina, and that known as the temple of Romulus. The first (transformed in the Middle Ages into the church of San Lorenzo in Miranda) was erected in honour of Antoninus Pius and his wife Faustina who was deified. Of it there remain the ten great onion-marble columns of the pronaos (narthex) and the side walls of peperino, topped by a fine marble frieze.

ARCH OF TITUS

The second, it seems, is dedicated not to the mythical founder of Rome, but to Romulus, son of Maxentius, who died while a youth and was deified by his father. The temple of Divus Romulus, of which the portal with its two porphyry columns remains, communicates with the existing church of Saints Cosma and Damiano.

The area surrounding the Forum Romanum is dominated by the imposing Basilica of Maxentius and the Arch of Titus. The Basilica of Maxentius, which is one of the greatest and most daring creations of Roman architecture, served as a model to the Renaissance architects for the building of the greatest churches and halls in Rome and the whole world. It was started by Maxentius and finished by Constantine, who defeated his rival before the gigantic building was completed. The basilica, designed like the others for meetings and business, suffered severe damage in the terrible earthquake of 847, apart from other damage. Its structure was studied by Bramante and Michelangelo for the building of the Basilica of St Peter's.

The Arch of Titus, which completes the peerless scenery of the Forum, was erected after A. D. 70 to celebrate that victory over the Jews which concluded with the destruction of Jerusalem. The Arch, which was restored by Valadier in the opening years of the nineteenth century, was also called " The Arch of the Seven Lamps ", because one of its reliefs shows the famous seven-branched candlestick from the Temple of Solomon, brought to Rome after the destruction of Jerusalem.

And so we arrive at the Palatine, (the name derives from *Pales*, the divine protectrss of pasturage) the hill of " square Rome ", which keeps Rome's most ancient memories and where we find a majestic group of monuments among the most notable of antiquity : the remains of the Temple of Cybele, the house of Augustus (wrongly called the house of Livia, Augustus' wife), wonderfully decorated with paintings, Nero's cryptoportico (a sumptuous underground gallery which

TEMPLE OF VENUS GENETRIX IN CAESAR'S FORUM

joined the Palatine palaces to the " *Domus Aurea* "); the " *Domus Flavia* ", that is, the Imperial Palace, the great stadium of Domitian, from the top of which one can still enjoy a fine view of Ancient Rome; the huge ruins of the palaces of Tiberius, Caligula and Septimus Severus, of the Temple of Augustus, and, finally of Agrippa's granaries at the foot of the Hill.

The Temple of Cybele, or the *Magna Mater*, is linked to a legend. It is said that in B. C. 206 there was, at Rome, a hail of stones, for which the Sibylline Books were consulted. The answer was that a mission should be sent to Pexinunte, in Asia Minor, to bring back the goddess's likeness in the form of a pointed stone which had fallen from the sky. The ship which carried the sacred stone gounded in the mouth of the Tiber; at this, the Vestal Virgin, Claudia Quinta, about whose virginity there were grave doubts, offered to free the ship to demonstrate her virginity, and succeeded in doing so only with her girdle. At the point where the Tiber joins the Almone, the image of the goddess was washed, together with other articles belonging to the cult, and then brought to the Palatine, where a temple was erected in her honour. Every year, on the 4th April, the anniversary of this event, the ceremony of washing the image of the Great Mother was repeated, with a solemn procession.

Before continuing our journey, we must turn our attention to the Via dei Fori Imperiali where, on the left as you look towards the Colosseum, there are, in fact, the imperial Forums. To the right is Caesar's Forum, built when the Roman Forum, owing to the increase in population, became insufficient for business and the administrazion of Justice. The temple erected in this Forum is dedicated to Venus Genetrix from whom the Gens Julia claimed their descent.

The Forums which can be seen to the left are those of Trajan, with the Ulpian Basilica (close to which are the great Trajan's Markets), the Forum of Augustus, with the temple

TRAJAN'S COLUMN

20

of Mars Ultor, the Forum of Nerva, or the Transitional, the Forum of the Peace, or of Vespasian.

Trajan's Column, which rises in the Forum of the same name, is covered with a bas-relief more than 200 yards long, in spiral form from the base to the summit. It has been rightly compared to an illustrated book, made of one huge parchment scroll that shows the glorious enterprises of the emperor Trajan in conquering Dacia. It is by the famous architect Apollodorus of Damascus. There are more than 2,500 figures grouped in many frames, and the effigy of the great emperor is shown more than 50 times. On the top there was a statue of the emperor in life-size, which was replaced in 1587, by order of Pope Sixtus V, by another representing St. Peter. Having admired Trajan's Column, Stendhal wrote, " It seems that the bas-reliefs are a perfect model of historical style; nothing is overdone, nothing is omitted. The movement of the figures is rendered with a majesty worthy of Phidias; it is the most perfect portrait the Romans have left of themselves ".

Legend has it that Pope St. Gregory the Great, considering the majesty of Trajan's Forum, invoked the liberation of the pagan Emperor's soul who had built it, and obtained this divine favour.

The Forum of Augustus was built to satisfy the vow of expiating Caesar's death in the noblest possible way. It was inaugurated in 2 B. C. with solemn festivities; a warlike parade which was followed by the slaughter of 260 lions in the Circus Maximus; in the Flaminian circus there was a battle of gladiators and a mock naval battle.

When one arrives at the end of the Via dei Fori Imperiali, in the Parco Oppio, one may see the ruins of Nero's *Domus Aurea*, the palace which Nero put up after the Rome fire of A. D. 64. After another fire, that of A. D. 104, the buildings of the palace were used for such public utility buildings as the Baths of Trajan.

Colosseum

Nero wanted extensive and wonderful gardens around his palace, and in the middle of the valley he created a deep lake surrounded by sumptuous buildings. The whole complex of the *Domus Aurea*, according to contemporary writers, was of such beauty and luxury as to astonish the Orientals who came to Rome. The space once devoted to the ornamental lake is now occupied by the Colosseum. In fact, the *stagnum* of the *Domus Aurea* was drained in order to build the foundations of the gigantic Flavian Amphitheatre, which is named after the Flavian dynasty, who built it with the idea of carrying out works of public benefit after the oppressions of Nero. It is the greatest monument of Roman civilisation which has survived fires, earthquakes, the despoiling of Renaissance times and the ruin of the centuries. It is the symbol of the eternity of Rome. It should be here remembered that the Venerable Bede, an English monk and doctor of the Church, one of the greatest scholars of the early Middle Ages, prophesied that, " While the Colosseum stands, so will Rome; when the Colosseum falls, so will Rome; but when Rome falls, the world will end ".

The name Colosseum, which took the place of the official one of the Flavian Amphitheatre from the most ancient times, derives from the colossal size of the building, though some authorities hold that the origin is different and derives from the bronze statue called the Colossus of Nero, 98 feet high, which rose, in fact, in the valley where the Colosseum is found. The statue was originally where the ruins of the temple of Venus and Rome are now to be found. The Emperor Hadrian, when he built this temple, ordered the removal of the statue into the valley of the Colosseum on the backs of 24 elephants. Even today, there is a small, square patch, paved with travertine, to commemorate the spot where the statue stood. It was melted down for money and arms during the Gothic invasions.

Whatever the derivation of the word may be, it aptly describes the grandeur of the structure, as can be seen; it is as high as a modern twelve-storied building and built of three tiers of eighty arches of travertine, surmounted by a continuous wall which has now largely disappeared. Of the gigantic building — begun about 70 A. D. by the wish of Vespasian and inaugurated by Titus with festivals and games which lasted for a hundred days, the structure and thirty-three of the arches remain.

It constitutes one of the most obvious witnesses to the building ability of a people supreme in this field. It should suffice to allude to the technical perfection which still astonishes people today, and which allowed, for instance, the flooding of the arena for the fighting of mock naval battles (*naumachie*), or the spreading of a huge sunshade over the 80,000 spectators, of the use of no less than 32 counterweight elevators for bringing the wild beasts from the underground part to ground level, and of raising a stout railing, attached to large beams, all round the arena during the hunting of the wild beasts. The most popular spectacle was that of gladiators fighting in pairs (sometimes prisoners of war, or slaves released to the impresario (known as the *lanista*) by cruel masters, or criminals under sentence of death who hoped in this way to save their lives). When one of them was so wounded as to be forced to yield, he asked for mercy hy raising his index finger. And the final sentence rested with the people; the waving of togas for mercy, the closed fist raised with thumb pointing downward (" thumbs down ") signalled the death sentence for the unfortunate wretch, who had to take up his arms again or be killed on the spot.

In the hunts (*venationes*), those under sentence of death were often made to fight. Although there is no historical evidence for the fact, it is said that many Christians suffered in this way. It is quite probable, however, that during periods of persecution, there may have been Christians among these, as those condemned to death. The celebrated words of St Ignatius of Antioch seem to show the validity of this

ARCH OF CONSTANTINE

theory : " I am the wheat of Christ, I shall be ground between the teeth of wild beasts, to be found again as the purest bread".

For that matter, the fact that Pope Benedict XIV (1740-1758) raised a cross in the Colosseum, declaring it sacred for the Christian blood spilled there is a proof of the tradition, although the desire to prevent the buinding from being used as a quarry for travertine also enters into this.

The solemn view of the Colosseum is completed by the Arch of Constantine. This is imposing and has great artistic value, as the most precious decorative reliefs of the Arch are of previous periods, of that of Trajan, Hadrian and Marcus Aurelius. It has also the other merit of representing historically the passage from paganism to Christianity. It is, in fact, known that the great monument with its three arches was dedicated, it seems, in A. D. 316 by the Senate and the Roman people after Constantine's victory over Maxentius at the *Saxa Rubra*, a victory which indicates the definitive triumph of Christianity, because tradition has it that it was obtained with the help of God. It is said, in fact, that Constantine, prior to the victory had a vision of the Cross surrounded by the words " *In hoc signo vinces* " (by this sign shalt thou conquer).

Not far from the Arch of Constantine is the valley situated between the Palatine and the Aventine, occupied by the Circus Maximus, the greatest in the Roman Empire. It was in fact, 650 yards long by 115 yards wide and its capacity, at the time of the chariot races, was 320,000 people. According to tradition, it was founded by the Tarquins, who chose the spot where the rape of the Sabine women took place. Even at the time of Romulus festivals with horse races in honour of the god Consus, protector of agriculture, were held in this zone. It was during one of these celebrations (called, appropriately, *Consualia*) that the famous rape occured, which allowed Romulus to find wives for his subjects. To return to the Circus Maximus, it was enlarged in the Republican period and adorned during the Empire under Augustus (who brought the obelisk of Rameses II from Heliopolis), Claudius and Nero, who afterwards set fire to it. It was Trajan who rebuilt it and, subsequently, new work was added by Caracalla, Aurelian, Diocletian and Maximian. Constantine had the idea of adorning it with a second obelisk brought from Thebes. The two obelisks are now respectively in the Piazza del Popolo and the Piazza of St John Lateran. The emperors would watch the shows from the Palatine. Even mock battles were organised there. A memorable one was that made in 46 A. D. by Julius Caesar, who reconstructed a battle with a thousand infantrymen, 600 cavalry and 40 elephants. A pleasant ancient fable is linked to the Circus Maximus, that of Androcles, the Roman slave who fled from his master and met with a lion in the desert, where he removed a thorn from the lion's paw. Captured and brought back to the Circus, he saw coming towards him the lion he had cured which, instead of tearing him to pieces, licked his hand joyfully and protected him from the other wild beasts.

The Circus Maximus is at the centre of a vast archaeologcal zone which comprises the Baths of Caracalla on the one side and, on the other, the district known in ancient times by the name of Velabro, the Forum Boarium (cattle market) and the Forum Olitorium (fruit and vegetable market).

The Baths of Caracalla were planned by Septimus Severus and inaugurated by his son Caracalla in A. D. 206. It rises in the immediate vicinity of the Via Appia (where in still more ancient times there had been a true artificial lake, called the Public Swimming Pool, useful for those who wished to begin swimming but did not risk themselves in the currents of the Tiber), and certainly owes its position to the wealth of waters in that zone. They may be considered as the greatest and best equipped baths in the world, able to hold 1,600 people, who could choose hot or cold baths, showers or steam baths. The internal decoration of the place was so rich as to recall that of oriental palaces; precious marbles, stucco work, mosaics and every kind of work of art served to embellish them.

At the present time, the ruins of the baths offer a marvellous stage for opera in the summer.

Near here begins the Via Appia, the *Regina Viarum* (Queen of Roads), opened in B. C. 312 and which goes from Rome to Brindisi; the stretch near Rome (which will shortly be included in a great archaeological park), with the Tomb of Cecilia Metella, the Circus of Maxentius, the Catacombs, sacred to the memory of early Christianity, the Quintilian Villa, is the compulsory rendez-vous for one of the finest walks that it is possible to go for in the neighbourhood of Rome. The road leaves the city through the towered Gate of St Sebastian, the most imposing of the gates in the city wall. It would be as well, here, to remind the reader that the Aurelian Wall, begun in 272 A. D. by the emperor Aurelian and nearly 10 miles long, is undoubtedly the most imposing monument in Rome, with its handsome gates of the Ostiense, Porta Latina, Porta Maggiore and Porta Tiburtina.

Let us now return to the Baths of Caracalla; but before pursuing our itinerary towards the Forum Bovarium, we must mention another imposing Baths — those of Diocletian, built between 298 and 305 A. D., whose remains are found near the Termini Station, and from which the Station takes its name.

In the zone of the Forum Boarium, can be seen the "Arch of Janus". The name is incorrect, as the monument has no reference to the god Janus, but to the common noun *ianus*, which means an arch with four entrances which cross and which, in this case, refers to the form of the building erected in the period between that of Diocletian and that of Constantine, as a place of shelter and meeting between merchants. Close at hand is the Arch of the Argentari, or silversmiths, erected by the money-changers and cattle merchants of the Forum Bovarium in honour of Septimus Severus and his family in A. D. 204. The Cloaca Maxima passes underground at this point. It is said to have been constructed by Tarquin the Proud, and begins not far from the Roman Forum, going towards the Velabro to flow our into the Tiber near the " Ponte Rotto ".

Here, too, is the so-called temple of Fortunae Virilis, rare example of the architecture of Republican times, next to it is the Temple of Vesta, dating from the time of Augustus and wrongly called by this name, because of its similarity of form to that in the Forum, but actually perhaps dedicated to the divinity of gates and doors (*Portunus*).

Not far away rises the Theatre of Marcellus, which was built nearly a century before the Colosseum. After the Theatre of Pompey, it is the first permanent theatre in Rome and served as a model for the Flavian Amphitheatre. It was begun by Julius Caesar and finished in A. D. 11 by Augustus, who dedicated it to the memory of the husband of his daughter Julia, who died young and whom he had adopted as his successor. The Theatre of Marcellus was inaugurated with great pomp and solemn festivities. A slight accident disturbed the ceremony. Suddenly the *sella curulis*, that is the ivory throne on which the emperor sat, broke and he fell. Amid the anxiety of the senators, the dignitaries and the people, Augustus rose, smiling and ordered that the show, which had momentarily been suspended, should continue.

The Theatre of Marcellus, which has three orders of arcades like the Colosseum, enjoyed its greatest splendour under the Flavians and especially under Domitian. This was the emperos who instituted special literary and poetic competitions during the festivals known as " quinquatrian ", because they lasted five days, and took place in the month of March in honour of Minerva.

About four centuries after it was built, the theatre was partly demolished to make way for the Ponte Cestius, and the ruins formed a kind of hill, which took the name of Monte Savello, a name which is still used for the zone, from the

PANTHEON

30

Savelli family, owners of the property in the Middle Ages, when it was transformed into a fortress. They were succeeded in this stronghold, which arterwards became a noble palace, by the Pierleoni, the Orsini and the Caetani.

In the centre of the area known as Monte Savello, we find the remains of the " Portico of Octavia ", erected in Republican times, rebuilt by Augustus after 27 A. C., who dedicated it to his sister, Octavia, and extensively restored under Septimus Severus and Caracalla (205 A. D.). The portico has a double arcade (originally it had a frontage of 129 yards and was 147 yards deep) and was originally intended to be a public promenade and with its ornaments of Greek sculpture and famous paintings, was a true museum. To the right of the mediaeval arch, carved in the propylons of the entrance to the Portico, there is a marble tablet with a Latin inscription saying, " Heads of fish longer than this marble are to be given to the Conservators up to the first fins ". The reference is to an ancient fish market (from which the nearby church of San Angelo in Pescheria (S. Angelo of the Fishery gets its name) and the marble served to establish the lengths of those fish whose head parts belonged by right to the Conservators.

The Largo di Torre Argentina is not far from here, where until the early years of the Papacy of Pius IX, the ghetto was situated. The name " Argentina " — extended to the whole zone where four republican temples were discovered between 1926 and 1930, attribution of which is still under discussion — comes from *Argentoratum*, the Latin name of the city of Strasburg, which was the native city of Alexander VI's Master of Ceremonies, John Burckhardt, who had a house there which is now the home of the Theatre Museum. It is interesting to remember that during the papacy of Julius II, John Burckhardt directed the ceremony of laying the first stone for the new Basilica of St Peter.

The Pantheon is only about two hundred yards from this zone. It is one of the most august, imposing and best preserved buildings of ancient Rome. It was built in 27 BC by Marcus Agrippa, son-in-law of Augustus. It is circular; the cupola, 118 $^1/_2$ ft in diameter, is 3 $^1/_2$ feet wider than that of St Peter's. After the fire of 80 A. D. it was restored by Domitian and Trajan and then rebuilt by the emperor Hadrian, who reproduced on the lintel the ancient inscription " Built by Marcus Agrippa when Consul for the third time ". The Temple was re-dedicated to the Christian cult in 609 A.D. by Boniface IV who, having obtained permission from the Eastern Emperor, Foca, who lived at Constantinople, dedicated it to St Mary of the Martyrs (*ad Martyres*). The Pantheon was the last stronghold of paganism, and the gratitude of the Pontiff and the Romans to the Emperor was such that they erected a column to him in the Forum.

The temple underwent a certain amount of mutilation during the Renaissance. Urban VIII took away the bronzes which faced the beams of the portico to be melted down and used by Bernini for the Baldachin in St Peter's. But the bronze recovered turned out to be more than necessary, and the remainder was used for cannon for Castel S. Angelo.

Raphael and various other artists were buried in the Pantheon. His tomb is in the edicola known as that of the Madonna of the Rock, so called because the statue of the Virgin has one foot on a boulder. Victor Emmanuel II, Humbert I and Queen Margaret are also buried here.

Near the Pantheon, in Piazza Colonna is one of the most famous and typical monuments of Rome, the spiral column of Marcus Aurelius, the twin of Trajan's column, but even more famous because it is in the very centre of Rome. It was erected to the memory of the emperor-philosopher in honour of his victorious exploits against the Sarmatians and the Marcomans (173-176) and was finished in 193. The column owes its preservation to the fact that, during the Middle Ages it was the property of the powerful monastery of S. Silvestro in Capite, which defended it against every abuse.

1. VIA APPIA ANTICA

2. THE ROMAN FORUM

CASTEL S. ANGELO

33

Another great building of the Campus Martius, 148 ft high and 295 ft in diameter is the sepulchre of Augustus and the principal members of the Julian-Claudian family, the Augusteo. Its summit was dominated by the statue of Augustus and on either side the entrance there were two obelisks of rose-pink granite, one of which, in 1587, was removed by Sixtus V to the Esquiline and raised in front of the apse of S. Maria Maggiore, the second being removed by Pius V in 1786 to the Piazza of the Quirinal, flanked by the statues of the Dioscuri.

Opposite the Mausoleum, on the Lungotevere, the *Ara Pacis Augustae* (Altar of Peace of Augustus) has been reconstructed in a pavilion. It was erected between B. C. 13 and 9 to celebrate the peace established by Augustus throughout the Roman Empire.

The first remains of the monument were found in 1586 in the foundations of Palazzo Fiano in the Corso and were afterwards kept at the Uffizzi in Florence. In 1937, excavations were again begun, in the face of grave technical difficulties, under Palazzo Fiano, to recover the other pieces. The *Ara* was rebuilt in 1938, on the occasion of Augustus' bi-millenium. On the travertine case of the building, the will of the emperor has been reproduced in bronze lettering.

On the other bank of the Tiber rises another famous architectural funereal monument, the Mausoleum of Hadrian (Castel S. Angelo), built by the Emperor Hadrian in 135 A. D. as a sepulchre for his *gens*. Originally the monument consisted of a great square base, on which rose a cylindrical, marble-faced body, crowned by statues and a green tumulus in which cypresses grew, similar to an Etruscan tumulus. The summit was finished off by a kind of large altar, on which rested a quadriga driven by the Sun (Helios) which was one of the Emperor's names (Publius Helios Hadrianus). The bronze angel even today rests on a Roman structure more or less on the site of the quadriga. According to the legend, in 590 A. D., while Pope Gregory the Great was conducting a votive procession over the *Pons Helios* to invoke the cessation of the plague at Rome, an angel passed over the top of the monument in the act of sheathing his sword, as a sign that the wrath of God was placated. The name Castel S. Angelo derives from this event.

In the Mausoleum were laid the remains of the Emperors and their families from Hadrian to Septimus Severus. In 270 A. D., when Aurelian built the new city wall, he incorporated in it Hadrian's Mausoleum, which subsequently suffered from siege and sack during the barbarian invasions. One may well say that Castel S. Angelo represents the history of Rome over twenty centuries. It was by turns fortress, state prison, Papal residence and, finally, in our own times, a Museum of the most important historical exhibits of the Italian Army. Among its most famous prisoners we may recall Benvenuto Cellini, who fled by sliding down a rope of knotted sheets from a dizzy height, Beatrice Cenci, Giordano Bruno, Giuseppe Balsamo, Count Cagliostro.

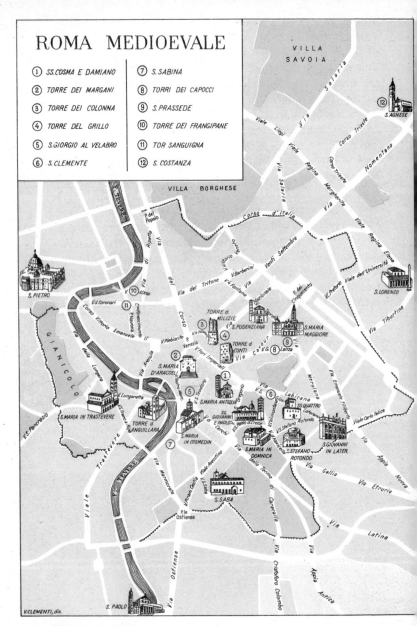

ROMA MEDIOEVALE

1. SS. COSMA E DAMIANO
2. TORRE DEI MARGANI
3. TORRE DEI COLONNA
4. TORRE DEL GRILLO
5. S. GIORGIO AL VELABRO
6. S. CLEMENTE
7. S. SABINA
8. TORRI DEI CAPOCCI
9. S. PRASSEDE
10. TORRE DEI FRANGIPANE
11. TOR SANGUIGNA
12. S. COSTANZA

V. CLEMENTI, dis.

MEDIAEVAL ROME

CHAPTER II

MEDIAEVAL ROME

THE EVIDENCES OF MEDIAEVAL Rome are less conspicuous than those of the ancient city, but they are sufficient to supply an imprint of the period running from the V to the XIV centuries and which includes the most disastrous period of Italian history and of that of Rome particularly. Christian Rome rose out of the ruins of the Roman Empire. A process of social transformation, as the Christian religion gradually asserts itself, in inverse proportion to the decline of the Caesars, is of necessity reflected also in the monumentsl development of the city.

This progressive change renders it difficult to separate clearly the topography of ancient from mediaeval Rome, nor does it make possible the assigning of an exact date for the end of one period and the beginning of the other. However, as a point of reference, one may take the Edict of Milan, promulgated by Constantine in the year 313, which granted freedom of worship to the Christians and ordered the restitution of confiscated goods.

Little by little Rome lost the lineaments of an imperial pagan city and acquired new graces from the domination of the Catholic Church. Christian basilicas rose on the remains of classical dwellings or pagan temples. The centre of life and activity moved from the Forum to the Lateran, seat of the Bishop of Rome. The Pontifical Curia took over the task of civic organisation. The Church of Christ took over the place that the Empire had deserted with its transfer to Byzantium and the religion therefore found the basis and pre-requisites for its great expansion.

But with the military weakness of the Roman Empire, came a succession of barbarian invasions which profaned the soil of the city. No longer held by the Alpine and Transalpine valleys, waves of barbarians swept down upon Italy and upon Rome. After the Goths came the Huns, the Vandals the Erules and the Ostrogoths. But Rome did not die. The power of the Church, even in the midst of these calamities gradually increase and when the Longobards of Desiderius threatened Rome, the Papacy found its secular arm in the Franks of Pepin and Charlemagne. The Franks themselves were foreigners, it is true; but when Charlemagne won himself the title of Emperor and was crowned in St Peter's on Christmas day, 800, the pre-eminence of Rome was re-established and the Western Empire restored.

With the proclamation of the Holy Roman Empire, the secular power of the Popes received a stable guarantee. There was accordingly a revival of art and architecture, walls and acqueducts were restored and new buildings erected. But a new invasion came only a few years later, that of the Saracens, who entered by the port of Ostia and came up the Tiber to the gates of the city. The walls held, but the barbarians sacked the countryside and robbed the suburban basilicas of St Peter and St Paul of all their precious ornaments. It was in these painful circumstances that Pope Leo IV, to protect the tomb of the first of the Apostles, surrounded the Vatican Basilica with a mighty wall which arrived at Castel S. Angelo, creating the present Leonine Wall.

The following centuries are characterized by fresh invasions, by the struggle between Empire and Papacy, by the growing power of the Roman barons, who raised towers and fortresses within the city, clinging to, and perching on the ruins of the ancient monuments. This is the height of the feudal period at Rome, which took the form almost exclusively of the division of the barons between those who supported the Empire and those who supported the Papacy.

The city is therefore divided into two clearly marked zones, the one, the Vatican, surrounded by its own fortifications, the other by a chain of forts of the feuds which, as the power of the Communes grew, became subjects over which the Commune attempted to assert its power. So the Capitol came to house a renewed Senate and became once more the centre of civic life, which acquired an existence of its own, side by side with the Curia and the feudal power. During the period of the divided Papacy, when the Papal residence was tranferred to Avignon, the baronial struggles became even more bitter. It is a period in which Rome lost much of its prestige, a revolutionary period which permitted Cola di Rienzo to proclaim himself tribune of the people, although it must be admitted that the basis of his inspiration was Italian, and to create the Roman Republic, after having in vain invited Pope Clement VI to return to Rome.

The fortunes of Cola di Rienzo fell quickly, the Popes returned with Gregory XI and the Jubilees of 1350 and 1390 finally pacified the Romans.

So long and densely packed a period of history, naturally had its effect on the art and topography of the city. But the spirit of Rome always succeeded in imposing itself, and the various styles (Byzantine, Lombard and Gothic) continued to feel a little of the classical influence and of the mastery of that architecture whose name of Romanesque, in fact, derives from Rome.

Then, in the XI century, a new imprint was given to the art of the time by the Roman marble workers, setting off the spark of a new art for the first time in centuries of barbarism, especially through the work of one family, that of the Cosmati, which produced, for four successive generations, architects, sculptors and mosaic workers of great worth.

These historical notes, although very compressed, seem essential to be able to start our ramble through the most significant monuments of Mediaeval Rome, whose presence is particularly noted in the areas of the Forum Romanum, the Capitol, the Quirinal, the Palatine, the Lateran, on the road which led to St Peter's and in Trastevere.

An example of a pagan religious building transformed into a church is offered by SS Cosma and Damiano in the Forum Romanum (entrance from Via dei Fori Imperiali), built in the VI century by Pope Felix IV, using the old library of the Forum Pacis. The Basilica which had its decorations completely renewed in 1632 by Urban VIII, is dedicated to the two Christian martyrs born at Cyrus in Syria, two brothers who are considered the patrons of doctors, as they exercised the medical profession. Their relics were discovered thirty years ago under the altar in the crypt, closed in boxes of silver and oriental wood. The various Popes had a particular devotion for this church, for many years celebrating the Whitsunday Mass there.

Another VI century church, indicated as the oldest and most important Christian building in the Forum, is dedicated to S. Maria Antiqua. It was restored and decorated with VIII century frescoes after the damage caused by earthquake. The church, which is an important and characteristic monument of Byzantine art in Rome, for its wall paintings, was rendered visible to the public again only in 1900, after the demolition of another church which was dedicated to S. Maria Liberatrice, and which had been superimposed in the XIII century.

Still in the Via dei Fori Imperiali, on the corner of Via Cavour, we find one of the most ancient towers of the Middle Ages. Of the 900 that existed in Rome at that time, only a few remain, as they were destroyed by the barons. The last blow was given by Sixtus V, who had many others pulled down to wipe out the memory of a brutal and turbulent period. At one time, these grim fortified buildings, besides being strongholds and fortresses, were patents of nobility, as the right to erect them was reserved to noble families. On this

S. Maria in Aracoeli

same road, therefore, at the corner of Via Cavour, we find the Torre dei Conti, once belonging to the Conti family. It was built at the beginning of the XIII century by Riccardo dei Conti di Segni, brother of Innocent III. It was erected on the ruins of the Forum of Peace. It was not a sign of nobility, but was built to defend the Papacy at an important cross-roads. It was, in fact, built with Papal money to a design of Marchionne, who came from Arezzo. After that of the Militia, it was the greatest in Rome, so much so that Petrarch, astonished at its great height, called it unique in the world (*turris illa toto orbe unica*). The earthquake of 1348 brought down the top two floors; it therefore remained ponderous but squat. It took its present form under Urban VIII.

There is an important mediaeval monument in the Capitol also, S. Maria in Aracoeli, built about the VI century on the ruins of the temple of Juno Moneta, where, according to the legend, Augustus had from the Tiburtine Sybil, the announcement of the birth of Christ.

The Church of Aracoeli was considered a political centre as well, in the Middle Ages; the magnates of the city often met here to discuss Communal matters. In 1250 it was rebuilt in Romanesque-Ogival style by the Conventual Franciscans, to whom it had been granted by Innocent IV. The fine staircase, of 124 steps, was built on the initiative of Cola di Rienzo, who inaugurated it in 1348, as a vow in thanksgiving for the Romans who had escaped the plague. Among the finest works to be seen inside is the tomb of Cardinal Matteo d'Acquasparta, General of the Franciscans, by Giovanni di Cosma. Every year at Christmas time, in this church, the famous exhibition of the Holy Child takes place, in the well-known Crib. It is a wooden image of the seventeenth century, carved from olive-wood from Gethsemane, before which Roman children run to say their prayers.

Near at hand, right at the foot of the Capitol, rises the fourteenth century tower of the Margani, a noble family whose members covered many honourable positions in the

TOWER OF THE MILITIA

43

Capitol and who are buried in the church of Aracoeli. The top appears to have been cut off. There are still Roman eagles cemented into the walls, which shows how Roman fragments, taken from ancient buildings, were used as ornaments in the Middle Ages.

Not more than 500 yeards away as the crow flies, beyond Piazza Venezia, near the Quirinal (in Largo Magnanapoli), the Torre delle Milizie, also called " Nero's Tower ", because a mistaken popular tradition claims that it was from here that Nero watched Rome burning while he played the lyre. In any case the fortress which, as we have said, was one of the most colossal baronial buildings of the XIII century, was built by Gregory IX about 1210. It belonged first to the Annibaldi family and then to the Caetani. Boniface VIII (Benedetto Caetani) made of it a well-furnished defence work against the Colonna family, his bitterest enemies.

The Tower of the Militia, overlooking the Markets of Trajan, rising behind the Villa Aldobrandini, leans noticeably as a result of the 1348 earthquake, which reduced it to its present height. Owing to the extreme height of its mass, it was struck by lightning every year, and its battlements had to be repaired many times.

Close at hand, on the corner of the Via Tre Cannelle, there is a Ghibelline tower, once belonging to the Colonna family, enemies, as we have said, of the Caetani. It is in brick, with six floors and six windows. At the base, in a marble frame, there are three fragments of classical friezes, supporting the heraldic column, topped by the crown and laurel wreath. The story of the origin of the Colonna family, according to a legend which has some claim to historical consideration, is very strange. The legend tells that a poor cattle drover, while taking one of his cows to pasture, noticed in the courtyard of a palace rising in the midst of a meadow, a column with a bowl full of gold coins on top of it. When he had recovered from his first astonishment, he was in the act of taking it, when an unknown voice shouted, " Let it

S. Maria in Cosmedin

alone, it's not yours!" Disappointed and afraid, he went away. But some days later, he went back to the column and this time the mysterious voice told him to take three of the gold coins, to go to the Forum and cast them on the ground, when he would find the proprietor of the money. He obeyed, and as soon as he had done so, there came a young man, of poor appearance, who gathered up the three coins. The drover then invited him to his home, and after marrying him to one of his daughters, took him to see the treasure of which, according to the mysterious voice, he was owner. Te young man went to get the treasure and became the progenitor of the powerful family which, in obedience to the tradition, took the name of Colonna (Column).

The Tower of the Grillo rises a short distance away, on the slope of the same name (Salita del Grillo). It originally belonged to the Conti family. It was built in 1223 and was nearly always Ghibelline property. In the XVII century, a period when it was restored and improved, it passed into the hands of the Marquesses del Grillo. The name of the Marquess del Grillo is famous in popular Roman tradition; he was a strange type of aristocrat, noted for his practical jokes and his eccentricity.

The Palatine area, too, has, has many significant witnesses to mediaeval Rome. It is sufficient to recall S. Maria in Cosmedin and S. Giorgio al Velabro. The first, whose name derives from the Greek κοσμέιν which means decorated (a word which here refers to the ornaments added under Hadrian I) is better known as "La Bocca della Verità" (the Mouth of Truth). In fact, in the narthex can still be seen the famous crude mask (it is really an ancient conduit cover carved to resemble an open mouth) which, according to mediaeval popular superstition, was an idol capable of discovering the lies told by anyone bold enough to put his hand in the mouth. The unmasking of the perjured person, according to the legend, was pretty violent, for anyone who has sworn a false oath and then put his hand in the mouth of the mask, received a tremendous bite. It is said that in order to heighten the supernatural value of the Bocca della Verità, a guard with a sharp sword was sometimes concealed behind it. Throughout the whole of the Middle Ages and during the first part of the Renaissance, the mask was cemented into the wall of the church. Only in 1632, when the legend had lost its power and had become only a means of frightening children, did the priest in charge of the church have it put in the narthex, where it remains to this day, giving its name to the surrounding area.

The Church of S. Maria in Cosmedin is a typical example of mediaeval building. There are noteworhy Cosmatesque works inside. It was built in the VI century on the site of the Ara Maxima of Hercules, over part of a imposing building formerly designed for the use of the imperial official responsible for the provisioning of the city, (*Statio Annonae*) and was enlarged and adorned by Adrian I in the VII century. He conceded it to Greek monks fleeing from the Iconoclasts.

A short way off, near the Arch of Janus, rises the church of S. Giorgio in Velàbro, also of the VI century and with stylistic characteristics very similar to those of S. Maria in Cosmedin. The word *Velabro* indicates the area between the Palatine and the Aventine, where there was a marsh in ancient times and where Faustulus is said to have rescued Romulus and Remus.

It is only a short distance from S. Maria in Cosmedin to the Aventine. We may profit by the walk to take a quick look at the churches of S. Saba and S. Sabina. S. Saba is a three-aisle basilica dedicated to the Cappadocian monk, Saba, organizer and head of oriental monasticism. It was built on the site of the home-oratory of S. Silvia, mother of St Gregory the Great. It was rebuilt in the XIII century on the site of a previous VI-VII century church, and contains a precious cosmatesque pavement. S. Sabina, called " the pearl of the Aventine ", is a typical V century Roman basilica and is the best example in Rome of this. It is dedicated to the Saint of the name who was martyred under the Emperor Hadrian, and was built by Peter of Illyria between 422 and 432, at the time of Pope Celestine I, on the site of a patrician house.

It is the only church which had from Pope Sixtus III (432-440) tha privilege of having a Baptismal Font, a privilege in those times enjoyed only by the Lateran and Vatican Basilicas. It was restored by Antonio Muñoz about 40 years ago; he gave the church its original ancient lines.

An extremely precious document of Christian life and history in its early days in Rome is given by the Basilica of S. Clemente, which rises in the little piazza of the same name in the Lateran district (between Via S. Giovanni in Laterano and Via Labicana). It is of the Constantinian period and was built over the house of Clement I, the third Pope after St Peter. To him, martyred under Trajan, the church was dedicated; it was known as *Domus Ecclesiae*, that is, the Papal residence during the times of the persecutions; after the Edict of Constantine, it passed to the Lateran. Gravely damaged during the Norman invasion (1084), the church was rebuilt by the initiative of Pascal II. The new building rose practically on the ruins of the old, so that it is composed of two churches, one on top of the other.

The upper church, basilican in form and of three aisles, divided by sixteen ancient columns with a Cosmatesque pavement and spendid mosaics, looks from outside like a typical example of Byzantine art, owing to its wooden door, the only one of the kind that is still preserved at Rome, and which belonged to the lower basilica. Inside, according to the ancient liturgical rules, the chancel is in the nave, on a higher level than the floor of the church, and divided from the congregation by two orders of Greek marble chairs reserved for priests. The ceiling is eighteenth century work, like many pictures by Sebastiano Conca, Giuseppe Chiari and Pier Leone Ghezzi. In the underground basilica a *Mithraeum*, with an image of Mithras (the Sun-God) has been found; the cult was widely diffused in the late imperial period.

Another very ancient church, destroyed by the Normans and afterwards rebuilt by Pope Pascal II, is that dedicated to Santi Quattro Coronati (The Four Crowned Sains), the four martyred marble workers, Sempronianus, Castor, Claudius and Nicostratus, who underwent matyrdom for refusing to carve an image of the god Esculapius. Because of this the church is of particular devotion on the part of masons and marble workers. It is in Via dei Querceti, near Via S. Giovanni in Laterano. It resembles a fortress; the surrounding wall gives the impression of a fort, and the bell-tower gives an authentic note of the Middle Ages. There is a delightful Cosmatesque cloister, one of the finest and most evocative works left us by the Roman marble workers, both for the luminosity of the marbles used and for the light arches borne on jewelled pillars.

And as we are on the Celian hill, it would be as well to recall that there are other characteristic mediaeval churches in this district: the church of S. Maria in Domnica, with the great IX century apsidal mosaic, the church of SS. Giovanni e Paolo, which rises in a little piazza that has, after recent restoration, become one of the most evocative in Rome.

To find two other mediaeval fortresses, we must go to the Monti district, in Via Giovanni Lanza, where, on either side of the road, there are the two Capocci towers, also called the Cerroni and Arcioni towers, from the noble families who owned them.

That on the right, which is 110 feet high, is thirty feet lower than the Tower of the Militia. Both were built with material from the nearby Baths of Trajan. Of the Capocci family, the last to own the twin towers, we should remember Giovanni Capocci, known as Capoccio, who defended the honour of Italy at the challenge of Barletta. On that occasion he was chosen, together with Giovanni Brancaleone, as herald to carry the challenge to the Duc de Nemurs.

The ground plan is square, the two towers have sharp corners — one is now comprised in the buildings of a convent (that on the right) — and once were part of a great baronial castle, dominating the whole zone beneath.

In the same district there are several important churches of which we should mention S. Prassede (St Praxed), a very ancient church rebuilt in the IX century, the date of the apsidal mosaics and the splendid church of St Zeno, and S. Pudenziana, which posseses the finest late IV century mosaic in Rome.

From the Esquiline we return to the centre. In Via dell'Orso, rises the Tower of the Frangipane, better known as the Tower of the Scimmia (monkey). This name, however, is of the seventeenth century. A rich family lived there at that time. It is said that a monkey, of whom the master was particularly fond, took a child of its owners one day to the top of the tower, exposing it between the battlements to the danger of falling. Parents and people gathered, imploring the Madonna to save this little weeping creature. The monkey was then seen to descend slowly the tower with the child in its arms, bringing home the baby safe and sound. From that day on, the parents had a votive lamp burning every evening before the statue of the Madonna that they had erected on the top of the tower.

As for the ancient tower, which is of brick, decorated with travertine, it should be remembered that Oddone Frangipane was born in 1040. He was afterwards proclaimed a saint by the Church, famous for his pilgrimage to Ariano, where the plague was raging. Here he had the opportunity to exercise his great gifts of charity with heroic devotion.

It is interesting, reading the legends, to know the origin of the name of Frangipane, who are said to descend from the *Gens Anicia*. It is said that a member of the *Gens Anicia*, Flavius by name, during the Tiber floods, while famine. was raging, went round in a little boat giving bread to the people who, as they recognised him, shouted " *Frange nobis panem*!"

S. Maria in Trastevere

("Share your bread with us!"). From this the name of
Frangipane came down to the *Gens Anicia*. To commemorate
this legend, a large silver loaf between the paws of two lions
was placed on the arms of the Frangipane family.

Not far from the Tower of the Monkey, at the entrance
to Via dei Coronari, is the Tor Sanguigna, which gave its
name also to the street, and belonged to an ancient Roman
family, the Sanguigni. With its top cut off and without
battlements, entirely in brick, the tower looks on to Piazza
Zanardelli, with its four windows, one of which is faced with
travertine.

On the other side of the Tiber, that is, in Trastevere, we
mention as significant of the monuments of Mediaeval Rome,
the basilica of S. Maria in Trastevere and the Tower of the
Anguillara.

Santa Maria in Trastevere is one of the first churches
in Rome to be officially opened to that cult. It was begun
by Calixtus I (217-222) and finished by Julius I (337-352)
on the site of a Veterans' Hospice (*Taberna Meritoria*). It
was rebuilt in the XII century by Innocent II. According
to legend, the foundations were laid in the very spot where
a fountain of oil sprang up at the birth of Chirst. It was repaired in 1702 by Carlo Fontana, who built the portico. There
is no doubt that it is one of the finest basilicas of Rome and
its beauty derives from the harmony of its elements, although
they are of different periods.

The Tower of the Anguillara is the only survivor of the
many mediaeval towers that rose in Trastevere. It is better
known by the name of the Casa di Dante (an institution
created in modern times by readers of Dante for the diffusion
of the Divine Comedy); it belonged in the XIII century
to the Anguillara family, a Guelph family and one of the most
powerful in Rome. It was Orso degli Anguillara who crowned Petrarch in the Capitol, placing the laurel wreath of the
Poets on his head on Easter Day, 1341. During the first
half of the nineteenth century, there was a picturesque Crib

S. Lorenzo fuori le Mura

in the Tower, with a background of the Roman Castelli and the inscription : " this tower, warriors' fortress, captives' prison, when the passer-by saw it, he retreated; but you, guests from every clime, enter and be glad. It is the cradle of the new-born God, the Redeemer of Peace ". At the beginning of the twentieth century, the Rome City Council bought the building and after restoration, dedicated it to the " Casa di Dante " in 1921.

It would be advisable at this point to allude to the major basilicas of S. Pietro and S. Giovanni, poles of city life in the Middle Ages; we shall speak of these later, but we must mention the three suburban basilicas, among the most important in Rome, of S. Paolo, S. Lorenzo fuori le Mura and S. Agnese.

Unfortunately, S. Paolo, on the Via Ostiense, was destroyed by fire during the last century; now it is completely rebuilt, but with its nave and four aisles divided by a forest of 80 monolith granite columns, it gives a clear idea of what the great classical basilicas must have been like.; attatched to it is the picturesque Romanesque cloister built in the late XII and early XIII centuries, smaller but more elegant than the contemporary one of S. Giovanni in Laterano.

S. Lorenzo fuori le Mura (St Laurence outside the Wall) on the Via Tiburtina is a combination of two churches of the V and VIth centuries respectively, joined in the XIII by demolishing the cloisters. It is noted for the mosaics, for its beautiful columns and for the rich Cosmatesque ornaments of the chancel (XII-XIII centuries).

S. Agnese fuori le Mura (St Agnes outside the Wall) on the Via Nomentana is a basilica of Constantinian origin rebuilt in the VII century, with very well preserved matronea; it has a very beautiful apsidal mosaic of the same period; close by there is the circular church of S. Costanza, of the IV century, former mausoleum of Constantina; daughter of Constantine, who was buried there in a great porphyry sarcophagus, now in the Vatican Museums.

CHAPTER III

RENAISSANCE ROME

I T IS NOT POSSIBLE to speak of Renaissance Rome without immediately thinking of the masters who were its principal creators, Bramante, Raphael and Michelangelo. To these must be adeed other names equally worthy of being recorded for their fame and the masterpieces they left. But the glorious trio strike the imagination more forcibly than any studied enunciation which tries to synthesise the character of an epoch, or reproduce the atmosphere of a golden century.

Even though it is not easy to set topographical limits within which to group monuments of a certain period, the genius of artists knowing no such limitations, we can follow a fairly orderly itinerary for Renaissance Rome.

It is in fact, through a series of fortunate circumstances which we shall explain, grouped for the most part into a very well-defined zone. This does not mean, however, that we shall not have to make some indispensable deviations, as several works of great importance are found outside what is usually called the Renaissance Quarter.

If we consider the zone between Ponte Umberto and Ponte Sisto, or rather the area comprised in the curve of the Tiber at that point, we shall find, in that tongue of land, a Rome that is a strange mixture of times, in that buildings once inhabited by Popes, princes and artists of the Renaissance, are now occupied by people who perhaps do not realise amid what treasures they are living.

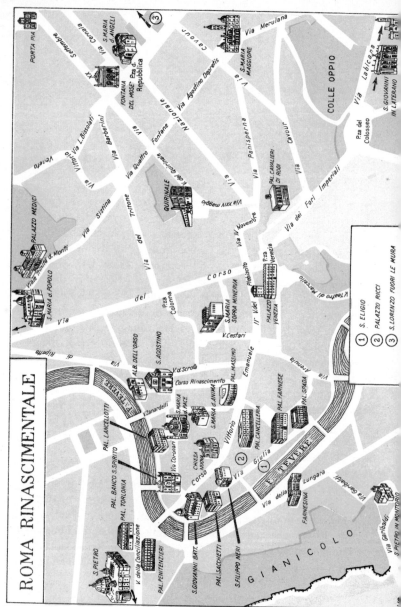

ROMA RINASCIMENTALE

RENAISSANCE ROME

To have an idea of the Quarter we allude to, we should take Ponte Vittorio as a point of reference, at the point where, with our back to Ponte Vittorio, it is joined by the left-hand Lungotevere (that opposite Castel St Angelo, of course). This point is an angle whose sides are the river and which closes the area in a kind of promontory, which is commanded from here. Parallel to the run of the river are Via dei Coronari, to the left, running to Piazza Navona, and Via Giulia to the right, running almost to Ponte Sisto.

This great triangle, is divided down the middle by Corso Vittorio Emanuele, in line with the bridge of the same name. These roads, with other adjacent secondary roads, form what is commonly called Renaissance Rome, a Rome which, for one reason and another, has been subjected to continual transformation from the first years of the fifteenth century. We are in the period when the Popes, on their return from Avignon, want their seat, which declined during the exile, to be great and magnificent. So the love for classical antiquity reflowers, as if by magic, together with the study of ancient monuments. The Renaissance of art follows on the Renaissance of Literature; and the Renaissance transforms just the most squalid parts of the derelict Mediaeval city. The frowning towers give place to campaniles and cupolas, the battlemented houses of the Roman barons to the elegant *palazzi* of Renaissance gentlemen. The very zone that must be crossed to reach the Vatican, now the permanent residence of the Popes, undergoes such a radical change that every trace of the Middle Ages gradually disappears.

Before entering this fabled zone, with its monuments, memories and traditions of the past, we must turn our attention to St Peter's. Even if this seems a disorderly way of proceeding, we must crave the reader's indulgence, as the seat of the Popes gave the fillip to the whole transformation of the adjacent quarter, and principally because the Vatican Basilica is, in fact, the most wonderful representative of the Renaissance period; the greater part of its building is owed

DOME OF ST. PETER'S

58

to that great Pope, Julius II della Rovere, who made Bramante open up the Via Giulia (Strada Julia), the widest of the first part of the fifteenth century, which leads, in fact, to the Vatican and which even today offers the vision of an epoch dominated by the personalities of artists who are among the greatest of all time.

Julius II took the daring step of demolishing the Basilica which Constantine built between 326 and 329 on the site of the martyrdom and burial of St Peter, as it was ancient and in a ruinous condition. He entrusted the work to the extremely famous artist Bramante, who prepared plans that for size and magnificence would overshadow all the churches in the world. On the 18th April, 1506, the Pope blessed the foundation stone of the present Basilica. The work of demolishing the great Sanctuary of Christianity won for the fanous architect the popular title of " Master of Breakage " or " Master of Ruination ". During this period was spread one of the most cutting Pasquinades, which deserves to be remembered as showing how pungent and pitiless is Roman irony, which, while admiring Bramante's majestic project, said : " When Bramante died, he went to the Gates of Heaven, but St Peter would not let him in, and reproached him for destroying the Church; The Maestro then said that he wished to enter Heaven only to be able to build more comfortable dwellings for the Saints and the Blessed ".

The great Renaissance Pope did not see his work completed. He died in 1513, a little before Bramante, who died under Leo X (Giovanni de' Medici, son of Lorenzo il Magnifico), who appointed to the direction of the great work, Raphael, with Giuliano da Sangallo and Frà Giocondo as assistants Then followed Baldassare Peruzzi and Antonio da Sangallo, invited by Paul III (Alexander Farnese) who called Michelangelo in 1546. The latter, old as he was — he was 72 — practically finished the work. The cupola, an authentic miracle of architecture, was designed by Michelangelo on the lines of Brunelleschi's in Florence Cathedral. After

Michelangelo came Giacomo Barozzi, known as il Vignola, and Pirro Ligorio and, finally, under Sixtus V, Domenico Fontana.

It was to the latter architect that Sixtus V (Felice Peretti) entrusted a project that Michelangelo and Sangallo had held to be impossible, that of erecting in the centre of the piazza the obelisk that the Emperor Caligula had brought in 37 A. D. from Heliopolis (thirteen obelisks were transferred Rome to Egypt in various periods) to adorn the circus built by him at the foot of the Vatican hill. The obelisk, which Domenico Fontana succeeded in raising with a great manoeuvre, that had something of the prodigious, held all Rome with suspended breath. It is enough to recall that for the scaffolding, a real castle, several buildings around the obelisk had to be demolished. It rose in the Piazza dei Protomartiri Romani, beside the Constantine Basilica, where a stone in the ground recalled the historic occasion. The preparations took four months; forty windlasses, 800 men and 140 horses were used. There is a legend linked to the daring undertaking, which was finished on 10th September 1586.

It is said that at the most critical point of the operation, the ropes were giving way through friction. At that exciting moment, while the crowd held its breath, anyone who had broken the silence would have been punished by sentence of death, as having caused distraction in this critical moment

Suddenly there was a cry, « Pour water on the ropes! » The advice was immediately followed (we don't know how), and the situation which seemed hopeless, was saved. The cry had been raised by a sailor from San Remo, a certain Bresca, who was among the labourers. As a matter of principle, the death sentence was decreed just the same, but when the sailor was led before the Pope to justify his action, he was not only pardoned, but the Pope invited him to express a wish. And he asked for the privilege for himself and his descendants, of furnishing the Vatican with the plaited palms for Palm Sunday. The privilege still exists, and the Bresca family presents the now famous palms to the Pope every Palm Sunday. Although many scholars, such as Carlo Cecchelli, after careful research, give little credit to the episode, which is said to be the transference of a similar event which happened with an obelisk at Constantinople, the legend is so widely diffused that no Roman, indeed no Italian, can be found who does not know the meaning of « Pour water on the ropes! ».

As we know, in the following century, the Basilica of St Peter changed its exterior aspect again, with the work of Maderno, who changed the Greek Cross plan into a Latin Cross plan, while Bernini built the immense, impressive Doric colonnade, which opens like two curved arms before the body of the Church.

* * *

But let us return to that zone contained by the sweep of the Tiber, which we have defined as " The Renaissance Quarter ". To follow a certain chronological order, that is, from the beginning of the sixteenth century to its end, it would be useful to go into Via dei Coronari and the adjacent streets; then into Via Giulia, profiting by the fact that the transformation of mediaeval monuments followed, with rare exceptions, this route.

The transformation was necessarily slow, the more so as we see, even today, examples of an architecture which can be described as transitional. The Albergo dell'Orso, in Via di Monte Brianzo, right at the entrance to Renaissance Rome, gives clear evidence of this. It represents the first tourist movement to Papal Rome, receiving a flow of important foreigners, foreign cardinals, nobles, ambassadors, ministers, prelates, artists, scientists and poets; there was a posting station for public and private carriages, and sedan chairs, carriages and horses to be hired for a tour of the city or for longer journeys gathered here.

FOUNTAIN OF THE TORTOISES

Before looking at Via dei Coronari, we think it useful to look at some of the neighbouring streets, to admire certain admirable jewels of Renaissance art. These are Via dell'Anima and Via della Pace, where we find, respectively, the churches of S. Maria dell'Anima and S. Maria della Pace.

S. Maria dell'Anima, built at the beginning of the sixteenth century for German Catholics resident in Rome, possesses a Renaissance facade, attributed to Giuliano da Sangallo, which is one of the purest Renaissance creations. Over the portal, once attributed to Peruzzi and now considered to be by Andrea Sansovino is a " Virgin interceding for two souls ". This church has one of the finest campaniles in Rome, attributed to Bramante, a campanile as slim as a minaret, crowned by the German eagle. Next to the church is the German Hospice.

The church of S. Maria della Pace (to which is joined a magnificent cloister by Bramante) has an odd and interesting history. It was once a little church called S. Andrea degli Acquarenari, so called from the water-bearers who filtered the sand out of the water of the Tiber and sold it for domestic use. On one wall of the little entrance portico, there was a painting of a Madonna and Child. The legend says that a stone thrown by a youth against this painting made blood issue from the Virgin's face. Pope Sixtus IV, who went there in solemn procession to venerate the miraculous image, made a solemn vow to build a splendid temple to the Mother of God if he should obtain the peace of Italy, greatly compromised after the Pazzi conspiracy of 1478. The prayer being answered, the Pope built on the site the magnificent church which is known as S. Maria della Pace. In about 1656 it was restored, by order of Alexander VII, by Pietro da Cortona who added the convex Baroque facade, preceded by a semicircular narthex with travertine Doric columns. In the interior, on the arch of the first chapel to the right, there is the famous fresco of the Sybils, a work by Raphael, carried out in 1514 and commissioned by the Sienese banker,

Agostino Chigi. The High Altar is by Carlo Maderno. By ancient tradition, Roman newly-married couples go before the picture of the Madonna della Pace to pray for family serenity.

Concerning the " Acquarenari ", it may be remembered that Ariosto, announcing in 1517 his arrival in the city (already in 1513 the poet had lodged at the Albergo del Montone, now the Albergo del Sole, in the Piazza del Pantheon) begged his brother Galasso in one of his satires, to prepare him a little lodging and to have the filtered water of the Tiber ready for his arrival. Apart from the historical curiosity, the episode shows how the lack of drinking water in the higher parts of the city had obliged the citizens from the Middle Ages on, to leave the hills and come down into the plain of the Tiber. Yet Rome was rich in Acqueducts. But the barbarian invasions of the V and VIII centuries had sowed destruction and ruin everywhere.

It was Sixtus V who made a development towards the higher part possible by starting work from the opening years of his reign (1586) for the bringing to Rome of a new source of water, called Acqua Felice after his own name (Felice Peretti). The aim was to supply the heights of the Quirinal and the Esquiline and the underlying plain. The monumental fountain of Piazza S. Bernardo is, in fact, the *mostra*(show) of the Acqua Felice. Like all the work of its architect, Domenico Fontana, it is majestic, but clumsy and cold.

Going back to the Via dei Coronari, which owes its name to the numerous shops selling images and rosaries in it at ine time (*corona* = rosary), it was created by Sixtus IV (*Restaurator urbis*), who called it *Via Recta*. Its original name was Via di Tor Sanguigna.

In this street, where can be seen the Palazzo Lancellotti, begun by the architect Francesco da Volterra and finished at the end of the sixteenth century by Carlo Maderno and the palace that Sixtus V destined for the Monte di Pietà (pawnshop), Raphael is believed to have lived in the house

3. TOWER OF THE MILITIA

4. CAPITOL

LATERAN PALACE

65

at Nos. 122 and 123. He also lived in the no longer existing Piazza Scossacavalli, in the palace rebuilt on the site of a building by Bramante, called the Palazzo dei Convertendi. The strange name of Scossacavalli ("jibbing horses") derives from a legend that while carrying sacred relics, the horses jibbed violently and obstinately at this point.

Around Via dei Coronari there are many traces of sixteenth century Roman life. It is sufficient to recall the Via dei Banchi Nuovi (Street of the New Banks), where there is the Banco di Santo Spirito (Holy Ghost Bank) — formerly the Mint —, a work of Antonio da Sangallo the Younger, and where Benvenuto Cellini had a workshop, together with the goldsmith Giovanni da Fiesole, for the working of gold and silver vessels.

* * *

To complete the picture of the Renaissance Quarter we must pass from Via dei Coronari to Via Giulia, the street which, as we have said, is linked to the names of Julius II and Bramante and which runs parallel to the Tiber from Ponte Principe Amedeo di Aosta to Ponte Sisto. The fortunes of this street are also linked to that of the Pope who succeeded Julius II, that is, to Leo X, who made Rome the chief intellectual and artistic centre of the world, calling there the main Italian geniuses of the time. Florentine by birth, Leo X had a particular regard for the zone inhabited mainly by his townsmen. In fact, in Rome, districts had been formed consisting of citizens from other parts of Italy. The Florentines of the State of Florence, comprising also the provinces of Pisa, Leghorn, Pistoia and Arezzo, were gathered in the " Ponte " ward, so called from the Ponte S. Angelo, where they built, in Via Giulia, the hospital for the sick from the continuous plagues. Naturally the election of a Medici Cardinal as Pope was greeted with great joy in the Florentine quarter, which the Pope went through on the 11th April

1513, under triumphal arches put up by the bankers of the city of the lily (Florence).

It was in fact by order of Leo X that the church of the Florentine Nation was built on the Via Giulia and dedicated to St John Baptist, the protector of Florence. Building of the majestic church was begun after 1519, to the design of Jacopo Tatti, a Florentine, known as il Sansovino. Plans and advice for this church were laid down by the greatest architects of the time, Peruzzi, Sangallo and Michelangelo. The church was also famous as being the stopping-off place of all the great Florentine notables passing through Rome; they had the right to a salvo on their arrival. St Philip Neri was rector from 1564 to 1575.

Right opposite the Church of the Florentines is Via del Consolato, opening into Via Giulia. It draws its name from a privilege granted by Leo X to the Florentine community in Rome, of having their own Consulate, to sustain their case. It was situated in the Palazzo del Consolato, in that street (Consolato = Consulate).

Going along Via Giulia towards Ponte Sisto, we find, on the right the Palazzo Sacchetti, wrongly ascribed to Antonio da Sangallo because of an inscription on the front (*domus Antonii Sangalli architecti*) which comes from another building. Others sustain, with more reason that it is by Annibale Lippi. At this point we find the remains of what must have been called Palazzo Giuliano or dei Tribunali, ordered by Julius II and begun by Bramante. Unfortunately, it remained an unrealised dream, owing to the death of both Pope and architect. There remain some marble seats which the Romans call the " Via Giulia sofas ". In this block there is the church of S. Biagio della Pagnotta (St Blaise of the Loaf), where Armenians officate and which draws its name from the ancient custom of distributing blessed bread to the poor on the day of the patronal.

Still in Via Giulia is the little church of St Philip Neri, dedicated to the one who, although he was Tuscan, was the

PALACE FARNESE

most beloved and popular saints of Rome, to the point where he deserved the title of the " Apostle of Rome ". St Philip Neri had two favourite walks, one was the little amphitheatre of the Janiculum, behind Tasso's oak, and the other was the farthest point of the garden of Villa Celimontana, where a plaque on a rough seat still recalls today, " here St Philip Neri talked of the things of God with his disciples ". The Chiesa Nuova (New Church - S. Maria in Valicella) is also linked to the history of this saint. It was built on his initiative and by the wish of Gregory XIII.

Almost at the end of Via Giulia, the rear prospect of Palazzo Farnese dominates the view, one of the finest palaces in the world, begun by Antonio da Sangallo the Younger and continued after his death by Michelangelo, the loggia with its three arcades being by Vignola, the terrace and the spacious arch which crosses Via Giulia and continues on towards the river.

On the other side of the Tiber is the Farnesina, built between 1508 and 1511 by the banker Agostino Chigi, and which afterwards took its present name because it was bought by the Farnese family. It was on this occasion that the idea arose — maginificent but never realised — of joining the Fernese to the Farnesina by a bridge across the Tiber.

Several amusing anecdotes relative to Raphael, the Fornarina, Michelangelo and the same Agostino Chigi, are linked to the Farnesina. It is said that when Raphael was painting the rooms of the Farnesina for Agostino Chigi (the munificient Sienese banker, advisor and financer of sovereigns and Popes, whose name is linked to the finest period of the Roman Renaissance), Pope Leo X asked the banker to " give back " Raphael as soon as possible so that he could continue his work in the Vatican. But the work in the Farnesina went on with exasperating slowness. The Fornarina (Raphael's mistress whose portrait by him is in the Palazzo Barberini) was concerned in this. The episode is recalled by the nephew of the banker Fabio Chigi, who says that Agostino Chigi

La Farnesina

70

" made the woman disappear for a time, as if she had been carried far away by other lovers, seeking at the same time to console the love-lorn painter with a promise to find her. He then pretended to write everywhere, to merchants who were friends of his, and to receive their replies, one of which at last said that she had been found and was on her way back. In this way he kept Raphael at bay for some time, during which the work went on; but seeing that he had fallen into boredom and melancholy for the long, vain waiting, he suddenly gave him back his lover one day, and to reconcile love and work, allowed her to stay in the house where Raphael was painting and pretended not to notice that they were living together "

One of them is told by Luigi Zanazzo, writer and Romanesque poet (Romanesque is the dialect of Rome). When Raphael was painting at the Farnesina, he writes, he was so ealous of his work that he did not want anyone to see it. Every time he went out, he told the guardian to be very careful not to let anyone in. At that time, Michelangelo was also in Rome, and there was a certain jealousy between the two. Michelangelo was dying with curiosity to see what Raphael was painting and, so as not to attract the guard's attention, he disguised himself as a seller of beans and sat outside. While the guard was not looking he slipped inside and looked at what Raphael was doing, then be took a piece of charcoal and drew a fine head on a wall in the same room.

Then he made off. When Raphael arrived — writes Zanazzo — he took his palate and brushes, and was astounded to find that fine head, looking real, on the wall before him. " That is Michelangelo's work ", said Raphael, immediately and without protesting, had the head left there, because a similar treasure should be kept.

This head can still be seen to this day. It is a charcoal drawing in the Galatea room and is considered the most valuable visiting card in the world.

As we know, the Farnesina was the setting for the Babylonian feasts of the banker Chigi, nicknamed the Magnificent. Even Leo X took part, on the 30th April, 1518, in a banquet offered in his honour. The stables which Raphael had designed were selected (they were demolished in 1808 owing to instability). The walls of the stables, not yet occupied by horses, were covered for the occasion with precious tapestries which also covered the mangers. There was a Belgian arras on the floor. At the end of the dinner, the Pope, who together with the Cardinals and the ambassadors who had been invited, was astonished by the abundance and exquisite nature of the food, turned to his host and said, " Really, Agostino, I thought I was on more familiar terms with you ". " Your former opinion is confirmed by the humility of the place ". replied Chigi, smiling respectfully and uncovering the manger to show that they were in a stable and not in a dining hall.

At this feast 2000 gold scudi were spent and at the end of the meal, as in other celebrated feasts of Chigi's, the gold plates were thrown into the Tiber at the end of the meal. But a malicious gossip writer of the day states that a large net had been carefully stretched under water level to recover these precious household goods.

At this point our itinerary through Renaissance Rome should end. But how can we fail to record other remarkable works carried out by the Popes who succeeded one another ay this time.

The first regularly planned piazza belongs to this period, the piazza of the Capitol, designed by Michelangelo, with the two lateral palaces and the fine, wide balustrade dividing it from Piazza di Ara Coeli; in this way he left his imprint on the renewal of the Capitol. He also placed the equestrian statue of Marcus Aurelius in the centre of the piazza (A. D. 161-180). It was brought from the Lateran for the purpose. It may be remembered that this is the only equestrian statue of an Emperor that has come down to us. It owes its preserv-

CAPITOL

73

ation to the fact that it was thought to be the statue of Constantine, the first emperor to embrace Christianity.

Another great work of Michelangelo, typically Renaissance, is the Moses in S. Pietro in Vincoli, the huge statue that should have been the principal part of the funerary monument to Julius II, ordered from the artist by that Pontiff himself, intending that it should be raised in the Basilica of St Peter. The guides generally show a slight scar on the right knee of the statue, supposed to bear witness to the fact that when the artist had finished the Moses, whose power of expression lacked only speech, he threw his mallet at it, shouting, " Why don't you speak? " Even if the authenticity of the story is extremely doubtful, it has its value as a popular critical appreciation of the Biblical figure, so eloquent in his terrible silence. In the flowing beard are hidden, visible only in certain lights, the altorilievo profiles of Julius II and Michelangelo.

According to Vasari, the Jews, men and women, in great crowds in pilgrimage to the Moses, venerating it as something divine.

To complete the wonderful picture of this golden century, we must not fail to mention Palazzo di Venezia, the first great Renaissance work of civic architecture, attributed to Leon Battista Alberti, and the Palazzo della Cancelleria (Corso Vittorio), built at the end of the fifteenth century with travertine from the Colosseum. The work was attributed to Bramante, but was certainly started by Andrea Bregno, known as Montecavallo.

The architectural crown of the Renaissance, however, is the Palazzo Farnese, which we have already mentioned (built, as well as by Sangallo, by Vignola, Michelangelo and Giacomo della Porta). To the end of the century belongs the Quirinal Palace, ordered by Gregory XIII for a summer Papal residence.

Other important civic buildings of the Renaissance are the Papal apartments in the Vatican and Castel S. Angelo, the Palazzo of the Penetenzieri, formerly of Cardinal Domenico

PALAZZO VENEZIA

75

della Rovere and of Cardinal Adriano da Corneto, now Torlonia, both in the Via della Conciliazione; the house of the Knights of Rhodes at the Forum of Augustus, the little villa of Cardinal Bessarione on the Via Appia, the Palazzo Massimo alle Colonne in Corso Vittorio Emanuele, with its curved facade by Baldassare Peruzzi; the Palazzo Ricci in Piazza dei Ricci, typical example of a painted facade, the Palazzo Spada in Piazza Capodiferro, notable for its rich ornamentation and the stucco decoration of the facade and the courtyard, the Villa Medici by Annibale Lippi in which the noble architecture of the garden facade is enriched by ancient marbles used as decoration.

We should also remember a whole series of churches which are museums of art, from the Gothic S. Maria sopra Minerva, attributed to the same architects as S. Maria Novella at Florence and rich in paintings and sculptures by Michelangelo; Mino da Fiesole, Filippino Lippi etc., to S. Maria del Popolo of the time of Sixtus IV but modified in the seventeenth century in which the names of Bramante, Andrea Sansovino, Pinturicchio, Mino da Fiesole and Raphael are linked to those of Bernini and Caravaggio, to S. Agostino, noble fifteenth century architecture with work by Raphael, Jacopo Sansovino Caravaggio; to S. Pietro in Montorio, with a sobre Renaissanc facade enriched by the " Tempietto " of Bramante which rises in the adjacent cloister.

The name of Michelangelo also comes to mind for the church of S. Maria degli Angeli, which he built out of the vast tepidarium of the Baths of Diocletian, and for Porta Pia, at the entrance of the great arterial road designed by Pius IV from the Quirinal to the wall.

This is the period of the building of those great arterial roads created with an exact idea of the city's future function and it is from this time on that the development plans of the City becomes a model for the whole world. It is sufficient to recall that the plan of Sixtus V realised the connection in straight lines of the tops of the Esquiline, Viminal, Quirinal

THE LITTLE TEMPLE OF S. PIETRO IN MONTORIO

and Pincio Hills and of the basilicas of S. Maria Maggiore, S. Giovanni in Laterano, S. Croce in Gerusalemme and S. Lorenzo fuori le Mura.

The Popes, when their position of supreme rulers of the Church had been established, radically changed the face of the City, making it again a World Capital. With the rebirth of the sense of universality, the destinies of architecture and sculpture, for two hundred years, in the whole of Europe, were decided in Rome.

PORTA PIA

79

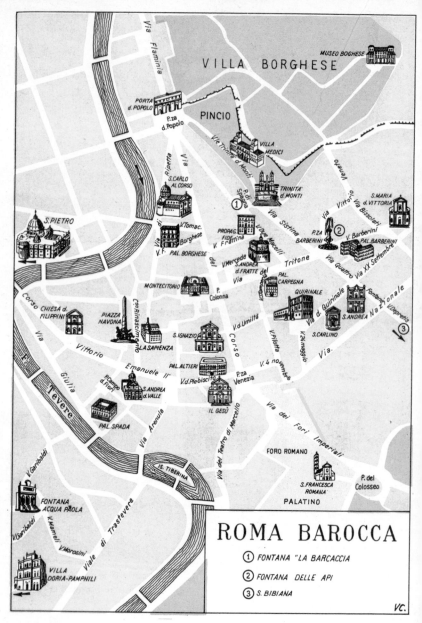

ROMA BAROCCA

① *FONTANA "LA BARCACCIA*
② *FONTANA DELLE API*
③ *S. BIBIANA*

BAROQUE ROME

CHAPTER IV

BAROQUE ROME

L ET US NOW GLANCE at Baroque Rome. First, what is the meaning of this word? What is its origin? It derives from " baròco ", a mnemonic term used in the Middle Ages by followers of Aristotle to indicate that type of syllogism in which the major premiss is affirmative and the second and conclusion are negative. (E. g.; All men are mortal; God is not man; therefore God is not mortal).

From reaction to Aristotelian pedantry, the word " Baròco " became in the common tongue a synonym for complicated reasoning, or captiousness. Applied to the art which began to develop in the seventeenth century, the epithet was used in disdain, to mean pompous. But if the Baroque style fell into heaviness and bad taste elsewhere, it found interpreters of genius at Rome, usually with a sense of proportion, who have left stupendous works, with an imprint of great magnificence. It is sufficient to name its principal followers : Bernini, Borromini, Girolamo and Carlo Rainaldi, Maderno.

They lived in the period following Sixtus V, who can be considered as its initiator, with the tendency towards perspectives and natural backgrounds revealed by the widening of the streets. A new tendency in which architecture is enhanced by the frame and background in which it is placed. Architecture develops a taste for perspective effects. It is the golden

COLONNADE AND FOUNTAIN IN ST. PETER'S SQUARE

age of scenography, which is the secret of the triumph of Baroque art.

An incessant building activity went on, grandiose, under the inspiration of Paul V (Camillo Borghese), Urban VIII (Maffeo Barberini) and Innocent X (Giambattista Pamphili), who, assisted by a group of great artists, left an imprint on Rome not less than that of the first Renaissance Popes.

The first majestic image of Baroque Rome is the great colonnade that surrounds Piazza S. Pietro, a universal architectural masterpiece by Gian Lorenzo Bernini, an artist rich in invention and output, who is the inspiration of the century and who gave to his production visions of grandeur such as Rome had not seen since Imperial days.

The colonnade, the unique vestibule of the Basilica, was built at the beginning of the seventeenth century, after Maderno had completed the new Baroque facade. It was Carlo Maderno who transformed the Basilica from Latin to Greek Cross plan, mainly to cover the space originally occupied by the ancient Basilica. It was one of Paul V's successors, Urban VIII, to consecrate the new Basilica on the 18th November 1626. It had absorbed, in its building, a mountain of travertine, brought on rafts along the river and unloaded at a wharf called "The Travertine Port" on the right bank of the Tiber between Castel S. Angelo and S. Spirito. Historians record the great confusion reigning in the streets of the Borgo quarter, caused by those immense masses of stone.

The town-planning aspect of the piazza (this modern term is well suited to Bernini's work) came twenty years later, under the Pontificate of Alexander VII. It was, in fact, begun in 1657 and finished in 1663. The piazza forms a great ellipse, 250 yards wide, dominated behind by the Basilica, which thrusts out, like two arms, the two half-circles of the great Doric portico, 17 metres long, forming three covered galleries. The artist explained that he had chosen this disposition as showing the maternal embrace of the Church to the people of the world.

The magnificent scenography is completed by two stupendous fountains, disposed symmetrically on either side of the obelisk, raised in the centre of the piazza by Sixtus V in the previous century. The one on the right had already been erected by Carlo Maderno, but as Bernini had to arrange the entire Piazza, he moved it into line with the obelisk and the one he had designed for the other side, and rebuilt it a few yards further forward to the same design as Maderno, only enlarging and sinking the basin. The one on the left was inaugurated ten years later. The two fountains, a fresh, lively note in the monumental solemnity of the place, reveal the artist even in their splendid plumes of foaming water which break into all the colours of the rainbow.

Other works in which Bernini has employed the infinite resources of his genius are the Baldaquin and the Cathedra of St Peter, both in the Vatican Basilica. The former, as we have said, was erected over the Tomb of the Apostle, of the bronzes melted down from the Pantheon; it was completed in 1633 by Bernini, replacing the traditional pattern of canopy by a decorative element of extraordinary ornamental effect, the latter, also of gilded bronze, adorns the apse, where four colossal statues with gold mantles (the doctors of the Church, St Ambrose, St Augustine, St Athanasius and St John Chrysostom), support the bronze chair within which is the chair upon which St Peter is supposed to have sat. It is a pure Baroque feature, with its wealth of gilded metal and its subtle play of light. But a wonderful demonstration of the scenographic ability of the artist is given by the Scala Regia, which is the official entrance to the Vatican apartments, after the bronze portals in the great right wing of the colonnade. It appears, in fact, more imposing and deeper than it really is.

During the seventeenth century Rome was enriched by an abundant supply of water through an undertaking of Paul V who reactivated a great acqueduct, that which Trajan had

FOUNTAIN OF THE ACQUA PAOLA

built to supply the city, and which had been destroyed during the Gothic invasions. The " Mostra " of what is known at Rome as " Acqua Paola " is on the Janiculum, in one of the most beautiful and well-supplied fountains erected by order of Paul V. It was built by Giovanni Fontana and Flaminio Ponzio, who used material from Nerva's Forum and even four granite columns from the ancient facade of St Peter's.

The fountain of the " Paola " water has also been ascribed to Maderno, but recent research has excluded any participation on his part in this work. The great basin in front, into which the water pours in such abundance, must have been used clandestinely during heat-waves as a swimming pool, for an edict of the time tells us that " it is forbidden to dive in, with or without drawers "

To meet the expense of the great work, Paul V put a tax on wine. This measure caused some discontent, as it seemed odd at that time " to make the wine pay to bring water ".

On the Janiculum we can see also an enchanting villa of the period, the Villa Doria Pamphili (also called " Bel Respiro "), built between 1644 and 1648 for Prince Camillo Pamphili, nephew of Innocent X, by Alessandro Algardi, who took his inspiration from Hadrian's Villa at Tivoli, from which the material was taken. It is a lesser sister of Villa Borghese, extending over a wide, steep terrain whose rises and falls have been exploited by the architect to obtain picturesque scenic effects with trees.

A superb example of Baroque architecture is offered by what is by many considered the most beautiful piazza in the world, Piazza Navona, which occupies the site of Domitian's Stadium. The name derives from the mediaeval " *Campus Agonis* ", which became, through succeeding transformations - Nagone, Naone and finally Navona.

This piazza constitutes living witness to the disagreement between Bernini and Borromini, who have each left imperishable imprints on the face of Rome. The lay-out of the piazza is owed to Pope Innocent X, successor to Urban VIII; as the latter had been severely criticised for his nepotism, the latter dismissed all the favorites of the previous Pontiff. So Bernini, who, under Urban VIII had been appointed architect to the fabric of St Peter's and " re-planner of the fountains and conduits of Piazza Navona ", fell on evil times. Borromini, on the other hand, who had worked under Bernini and had more than one brush with him, was appointed in his place.

In spite of all this, the finest work in Piazza Navona, a true masterpiece, was carried out by Bernini just the same. In fact, when Innocent X proclaimed a great competition among all the architects of the time for a design for the monumental fountain, excluding Bernini, the latter did not give in, and succeded in beating his rival. He was helped by the fact that Innocent X did not like the design presented by Borromini. So Bernini succeeded in his intention. There are different versions of the story, but the most probable is that told by Bernini's son, Domenico, in " The life of the Cavalier Gian Lorenzo ". Prince Niccolò Ludovisi, nephew of Innocent X, as he was enthusiastic about the sketch for the fountain that he had seen in Bernini's studio, had the model sent to him and left it well in view in one of the rooms in Palazzo Pamphili, so that the Pope could not help seeing it as he passed by. In fact, Innocent X, after an excellent dinner with his sister-in-law (Donna Olimpia Pamphili, whose daughter, Costanza Camilla, Prince Ludovisi had married), passed through the next room and found the bold model before him and was forced to exclaim, " This model can only be by Bernini and this trick by Prince Ludovisi. And we shall have to use him, in spite of those who do not wish it, for to avoid putting his works into operation, one must avoid seeing them ".

And Bernini, now already fifty years old, laid the foundation stone in February 1648. The fountain of the Four Rivers was completed in 1651. In the obelisk, which came

FOUNTAIN OF THE RIVERS AT PIAZZA NAVONA

from the Circus of Maxentius and which rises boldly in the midst of the four rivers, is reflected once more the concept of Sixtus V of exalting religion with the trophies of antiquity. The gigantic statues that represent the principal rivers from the four parts of the world (Nile, Ganges, Danube and Rio della Plata) symbolise the universality of the Church. It is said, but the story is apocryphal, that Bernini gave the statue in front of Borromini's facade of S. Agnese, an aspect of horror as a criticism of the irregularity of the work. This is very original, however, and contributes greatly with its gently curving lines, to the incomparable scenography of the piazza. Borromini's supporters, referring to the critical gestures of the statues of the rivers, explained that the statue of the saint that dominates the church seems to be reassuring the Nile statue, telling him not to be afraid, the facade will not fall. This is imagination, however, as the fountain did not exist when the church was built.

But, to return to the fountain, it is said that on the day of the inauguration (8th June 1651) Innocent X was told by Boromini that the water would not flow. Hearing of this, Bernini kept the cocks closed on purpose. The Pope, admiring the work, could not help saying that, as there was no water, it could not be considered ¦a fountain. And Bernini replied that he would need a good deal of time to solve that problem. But while the Pope was preparing to leave the piazza at the head of his magnificent procession, there was a sudden splashing of spouting water. Bernini had signed to his men to open the cocks. Innocent turned round delightedly at the sound of the splashing and said to Bernini, " You always act as you are, and with this unlooked-for mirth you have added ten years to Our life ".

At the two ends of the piazza, the fountain of the four rivers being in the middle, there are two other fountains, occupying the site of two basins put there at the end of the sixteenth century. One, the fountain of Neptune, was decorated with statues at the end of the last century; the other, called the fountain of the Moor (del Moro), had the statue of that name added by Giovanni Antonio Mari after a sketch by Bernini : it represents a Triton holding a dolphin, and it has the features of an Ethiopean, hence the name.

In the seventeenth century, by closing the the main outlet near this fountain, it was possible to flood the piazza in less than two hours. A diarist writes that in the month of August, when the sun was at its hottest, on Saturday and Sunday, the famous drain known as that of S. Giacomo degli Spagnoli, was closed, the outlets of Bernini's fountain were blocked, so that the water ran down the steps and over the piazza, which being slightly inclined, forms a long bowl. The people, continues the diarist, croweed round to watch, especially on the steps of S. Agnese. The nobility, on those days, instead of going to the Corso, went round and round the lake in carriages and watched from the windows of the palazzi that gave on the piazza. The carriages were festively decked out and those of nobles and prelates were followed by hordes of boys, making an infernal racket, rather similar to that which in our own day they make on the night of 6th January, the Epiphany. There are edicts of the period forbidding people to enter the water without shoes, and still less naked, " under the pain of three strokes of the scourge ". The lake lasted until a few years before 1870.

Still from chronicles of the time we learn of the initiative of Innocent X for the total magnificent laying-out of Piazza Navona. They speak of the grandiose Palazzo Pamphili (to which family the Pope belonged) whose presence in the Piazza, to the left of S. Agnese, inspired the Pope to give it a magnificent frame. The building is the work of the architect Girolamo Rainaldi. The vault of the gallery in the palace has a great fresco by Pietro da Cortona.

We recall three other significant Baroque monuments, Palazzo Spada, the church and Oratory of the Philippines, the Sapienza, Palazzo Borghese, S. Carlo al Corso, S. Andrea della Valle, the Gesù, S. Ignazio, S. Maria della Vittoria and the internal face of Porta del Popolo.

Palazzo Spada, in Piazza Capodiferro is of the Renaissance but was restored by Borromini, whose " perspective gallery " has become famous; this seems much longer than it really is, due to an optical illusion based on light, a rising pavement, and progressively diminishing columns. At the end there is a statue of Mars brandishing a sword. To the visitor, Gallery and statue seem imposing, but as one goes through, one notices that they gallery is no more than seven yards long and the statue no more than three feet high.

The Chiesa Nuova, built between the end of the sixteenth century and the first years of the seventeenth, is a typical Baroque church, to whose decoration the principal artists of the time contributed, from Rubens to Pietro da Cortona, Maratta, Guercino, Baroccio.

The nearby Oratory of the Philippines, also called the Sala Borromini (Piazza della Chiesa Nuova) is also a work of Bernini's great rival, who employed his bizarre genius particularly on the concave facade.

The Sapienza, the ancient Roman University founded in 1303 by Boniface VIII, has several embellishments by Giacomo della Porta, who carried out suggestions of Michelangelo, and Borromini. The latter, it is said, built the church of S. Ivo in a most original way, turning into a tribute to the reigning Pope. In fact, the church which dominates the wide, handsome courtyard of the Sapienza, with its concave facade, has been built so as to imitate, with its strange plan of the cupola and the odd lantern, the shape of Urban VIII's heraldic bee. Borromini also built the fine library, with its elegant bookshelves, for Alexander VII (it is therefore called the Alexandrine Library). It has now been tranferred to the Città Universitaria.

Palazzo Borghese, between Via Ripetta and Piazza Fontanella di Borghese, in late Renaissance style, which was bought by Paul V Borghese, has certain Baroque embellishments by, particularly, Carlo Rainaldi. The Church of S. Carlo al Corso, which Pietro da Cortona seems to have completed about 1668, with its very elegant cupola, is by Onorio Longhi and is the church of the " Lombard Nation ".

S. Andrea della Valle, built between 1591 and 1655, is one of the largest Baroque churches in Rome and has the largest cupola after that of St Peter's. The architecture is by Carlo Maderno, while the facade is by Carlo Rainaldi; the paintings in the major chapel and the apse are by Mattia Preti and Domenichino.

The Gesù and S. Ignazio, the major Jesuit churches of Rome, were built in different periods, but the magificent interior decorations are pure Baroque. In the Gesù, started in 1568 by Vignola and continued by Giacomo della Porta, the frescoes vault by Baciccia of the second half of the seventeenth century, together with the extremely rich chapel of S. Ignazio to the design of Andrea Pozzo, should be particularly noted. In S. Ignazio, with its facade by Algardi, the ceiling is a masterpiece of perspective virtuosity by the same Fratel Pozzo, who has created an immense pictorial church arising out of the nave of the real one. The chapel of S. Luigi Gonzaga should also be noted for its richness.

S. Maria della Vittoria, with its façade by B. Soria and interior by Maderno, is to be particularly remembered for the " Saint Theresa in Ecstasy " by Bernini, which contains the whole essence of Baroque sculpture.

Also the monumental Porta del Popolo, corresponding to the ancient Porta Flaminia, has notable Baroque elements. The internal facade, in fact, was added by Bernini on the occasion of Queen Christina of Sweden's arrival in Rome. Christina had a great religious crisis that induced her to embrace Catholicism and abdicate in favour of her cousin, Charles Gustav (Charles X). Fearing the revenge of her fellow countrymen, she came to Rome in 1655, where she was received with great honour by Pope Alexander VII. Her official entry into the city is famous, riding on a white horse through

FOUNTAIN OF THE SEA-HORSE AT VILLA BORGHESE

the Porta del Popolo, with a splendid procession and great crowds of people.

Leaving Piazza del Popolo (already replanned by Sixtus V who had the obelisk raised there and which two centuries after was to become a neo-classical masterpiece by Valadier), we go towards Villa Borghese, begun in the first years o the seventeenth century under the Pontificate of Paul V. The enterprise was undertaken by the nephew of this Pope, Cardinal Scipione Caffarelli Borghese (son of a sister of Paul V), to whose illustrious patronage of the arts — he was called " the delight of Rome " — are owed many works of the period. It is enough to say that it was Cardinal Scipione Borghese to recognise the budding genius of Bernini, to protect him and launch him.

We therefore owe to Cardinal Scipione the building of the classical Villa Pinciana, where he gathered, in the gardens and in the Palace (built by Giovanni Vasanzio between 1613 and 1615), a collection of wonderful works of art. He did not desire a dwelling, but a house of delights for himself and his friends, where he qathered the finest works of art. The collection now forms the nucleus of the Borghese Museum and Gallery, which houses such masterpieces of Bernini's as the Apollo and Daphne, the " Naked Truth revealed by Time ", the David, the busts of Scipione Borghese, and such stupendous pictures of Raphael as the Deposition, paintings by Caravaggio, sculptures by Antonio Canova.

From Villa Borghese, going down towards Trinità dei Monti, we find the Villa Medici, built, as we have seen, in the second half of the sixteenth century by Annibale Lippi. The villa, now seat of the French Academy in Rome, is linked to an episode of Queen Christina's stay in Rome. The ball which adorns the fountain before the villa is no less than the cannon ball which she had fired from a mortar on Castel S. Angelo. Traces may still be seen on the iron door of the façade.

VILLA MEDICI

95

The villa dominates Trinità dei Monti, beneath which, at the foot of the monumental staircase, in Piazza di Spagna, there is a curious fountain often wrongly attributed to Bernini, but in fact by his father, Pietro Bernini, the " Barcaccia ". It is said that the fountain was put there to commemorate a flood of the Tiber, when the retreating waters left a boat high and dry at that point.

In this area there are two other significant monuments of Baroque Architecture, that is, the Palazzo di Propaganda Fide (in the street of the same name leading into Piazza di Spagna), and the Church of S. Andrea delle Fratte.

The first, of trapezoidal plan, is a joint work of Borromini and Bernini, author of the Piazza di Spagna façade, The Via Propaganda façade, including the church of the Three Kings characterized by a flowing scenography of concave windows and architraves, with heavy cornices, is Borromini's work.

Not far away, in the street of the same name, there is the church of S. Andrea delle Fratte, restored by Borromini. It was the national church of Scotland, of the XII century. Borromini added the bold campanile and the high, majestic cupola. The origin of the church's name is to be found in the word " fratte " - hedges. In fact, the church was in the open country when it was built.

There is other work by Borromini in Palazzo Carpegna, now the National Academy of St Luke, in Via della Stamperia. He built there a curious S-shaped ramp, which allowed one to reach the top floor on horseback.

From here it is easy to reach the *Quirinal*, a hill which over its whole area has wonderful late Renaissance and Baroque features. We shall mention the Palazzo Quirinale and the Palazzo Barberini.

At the Quirinal Palace, a huge building begun in 1574 by Gregory XIII on the site of a villa belonging to Cardinal Ippolito d'Este, Flaminio Ponzio, Mascherino, Domenico Fontana, Carlo Maderno, Bernini and Ferdinando Fuga, all worked at different periods. It was the last-named who

5. PIAZZA NAVONA

6. TREVI FOUNTAIN

PALACE QUIRINAL

97

completed the magnificent piazza from which a splendid viw of the city, dominated by the cupola of St Peter's may be enjoyed. In the centre there is one of the finest fountains in Rome, that of the Dioscuri, originally a sixteenth century work, but which has had several successive modernisations, built with the colossal statues of Castor and Pollux found in the ruins of the nearby Baths of Constantine. For this reason the quarter is called " contrada Caballa " and subsequently " Monte Cavallo " (the hill of the horses). On the front of the Palazzo Quirinale, Flaminio Ponzio's portal, carried out by order of Paul V, stands out. To Paul V is also owed the Pauline Chapel, as large as the Sistine Chapel in the Vatican, and the gardens, which are still carefully kept.

Near the piazza rises S. Andrea al Quirinale (also called S. Andrea a Monte Cavallo), a favourite work by Bernini, which, in the elegance of its elliptical plan and the precious nature of its ornamentation gives the measure of his genius.

It is true that Urban VIII Barberini was criticised for his nepotism and that his depredations among the monuments of ancient Rome to build the Palazzo delle Quattro Fontane produced the pasquinade " *Quod non fecerunt barbari, fecerunt Barberini* " (the barbarians began it, and the Barberini finished it off), but these accusations appear irrelevant when one considers the result : Piazza Barberini, Palazzo Barberini with the adjoining theatre, the Triton fountain, the Fountain of the Bees, etc.

The art of the best artists of the time (Maderno, Borromini, and Bernini), gave to Palazzo Barberini all the inspired elegance of the Baroque. Built on the northern slopes of the Quirinal hill, on the ruins of the Sallustian Circus, with material from the Colosseum, the Pantheon and other ancient monuments, the building, unique in its environmental decoration, bears witness to the magnificence of the Barberini family. Modern opera saw its birth in the theatre of this palace, which has all the features and grandeur of a royal

S. Andrea al Quirinale

palace, with the performance of a comedy written by a prelate, Giulio Rospigliosi (afterwards Clement IX), " S. Alessio ", set to music by Stefano Landi.

In the middle of the piazza there is the elegant, slim and upthrusting fountain of the Triton, by Bernini, who exulted over the difficulty of producing it. In fact, he had only a thread of water to use for the play. So he decided upon that Triton, with his face turned to the sky, both arms raised to hold a conch to his mouth; he blows violently through this conch, spouting up a high jet that falls into the two open valves of another conch. It is a masterpiece. On this point we may remember the verses of D'Annunzio, " Over Piazza Barberini / the clear sky opens, sapphire / the Triton of Bernini / raises his jet like a sugar-stick " or those of Belli, " Go and see what kind of mane / of hair the Triton's grown. "

Another fountain of Bernini's is that of the Bees, once on the corner of the Strada Felice (now Via Sistina) and then taken down and moved to the beginning of Via Veneto. The bee is the heraldic device of the Barberini family, and the water is spurted by three large bees into an open bivalve conch, according to the notion of all the fountains of the period it was used also as a drinking trough for horses. In fact, the Latin inscription, still quite clear, says, " Urban VIII, Pontifex Maximus, having built a fountain for the public ornament of the City (that of the Triton), built this fountain apart for the convenience of private individuals. In the year 1644, the XXI of his reign."

At the beginning of the Via del Quirinale is the church of S. Carlino, by Borromini, ingeniously planned in the dimensions of one of the pillars of St Peter's. In it, Borromini was able to give full play to the whimsicalities of his creative genius.

To complete our itinerary, we must get to the Stazione Termini where, in Via Giolitti, there is the church of S.

TRITON FOUNTAIN

Bibiana (the Roman martyr flogged to death for her faitih under Julian the Apostate), which was restored by Bernin for Urban VIII. It is attractive for Bernini's façade and paintings by Pietro da Cortona. On the altar is the famous statue of S. Bibiana by Bernini on the altar. Leaning on a column, the saint holds in her hand the palm of triumph conceded by her martyrdom.

Going down to the Via dei Fori Imperiali through Via Cavour, we find an example of Baroque art in the church of S. Maria Nova, called also S. Francesca Romana, built on the site of a previous church erected by Paul I on the ruins of the Temple of Venus and Rome. In 1426, S. Francesca Romana (Francesca Bussi dei Ponziani, canonised in 1608) founded the Congregation of the Oblates in this church. The façade of the church dates from the canonisation and is by C. Lambardi (1615). The great polychrome marble confession is to a design by Bernini. On the 9th March of every year, the day of S. Francesca Romana, patroness of motorists, cars stop between the church and the Colosseum for benediction.

Passing to Piazza Venezia and going through Via del Plebiscito, we may see Palazzo Altieri, in the splendour of its sombre seventeenth century architecture. Not far away, in Piazza della Minerva we find yet another significant work by Bernini, that strange, jocund, exceedingly patient elephant that carries balanced upon his back one of the Egyptian obelisks found in the zone. The Romans have christened him " Minerva's chick " as if to flatter the patient animal.

Palazzo Montecitorio, seat of the Chamber of Deputies since 1870, is also a Baroque work. It was started by Bernini in 1650 for the Ludovisi family, continued under the same Pope Innocent X for the Pamphili, and completed by Carlo Fontana for Innocent XII, who used it for the Tribunals. Of Bernini's we have the ground plan and the idea of adding to the majesty of the façade by curving it.

S. Maria sopra Minerva

With the Palace of the Parliament, we end our itinerary through Baroque Rome, of which we have indicated only the most significant monuments. In fact, one might say that there is no work, even if very ancient, that does not show traces of seventeenth century art through some subsequent restoration.

CHAPTER V

EIGHTEENTH CENTURY AND NEO-CLASSICAL ROME

I T MIGHT APPEAR illogical and contradictory to join
eighteenth century and neo-classical Rome together
in one chapter and one itinerary. In fact, the two
periods, as far as art generally is concerned are in complete
contrast. The art of the eighteenth century, that is to say
Rococo (from " rocaille ", a rock introduced into France
as the predominating element in the decoration of buildings,
fountains, gardens and villas) is a continuation of Baroque;
while Neo-Classical which gained hold in Europe at the end
of the eighteenth and beginning of the nineteenth centuries,
signifies a return to ancient and classical forms, and therefore
a reaction against Rococo, considered as the final phase of
Baroque development.

But the sudden passage from one style to the other is not
found in Rome as in other parts of Italy and in Europe gene-
ally. Eighteenth century Roman architecture, for instance
remains majestic and seems to foreshadow the advent of neo
classicism without making excessive concessions to the grace-
ful taste of Rococo. The return to classical balance may be noted
in Rome for the last part of the eighteenth century and pre-
cedes the advent of the new style. Significant examples are
offered by the architects Ferdinando Fuga and Alessandro
Galilei. The former built the atrium and façade of S. Maria
Maggiore under Pope Benedict XIV (Lambertini), and the

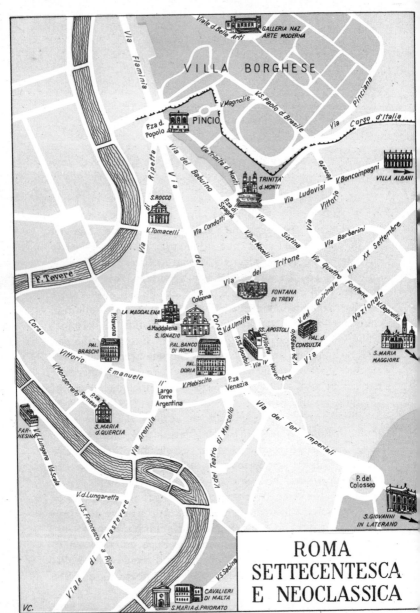

EIGHTEENTH CENTURY AND NEO-CLASSICAL ROME

latter, the façade of S. Giovanni in Laterano for Clement XII (Corsini) in 1736.

They are basically the first masters of that neo-classic style, which gained hold especially during the period of the French Revolution and which Napoleon made his own, elevating it to the official style of his regime under the name of " Empire ", and of which Giuseppe Valadier was the felicitous interpreter, with the layout of Piazza del Popolo and the stupendous Pincio promenade.

However, the strongest imprint to the Neo-Classical style was given in sculpture by Antonio Canova, who arrived from Venice and became aware of the voices of his time; Herculaneum and Pompei had come to light some scores of years before, and he drew on the perennial and revivifying spring of antiquity. He was a living emulation of the Greeks. In his hands, marble became soft, pulsing flesh and the classical spirit was affirmed through superb sculptures which gave their imprint to a whole epoch.

Beginning our itinerary through eighteenth century and Neo-Classical Rome, we shall try to observe a certain chronological order, presenting the monuments in the order of their creation.

Therefore we shall begin from S. Giovanni in Laterano, whose monumental façade, festive but balanced with two great porticos, one on top of the other, crowned by an attic and fifteen gigantic statues, is by Galilei. Also the Corsini chapel, dedicated to S. Andrea Corsini, by the same hand, is a spendid example of early eighteenth century art. Entirely faced in marble, in which pastel tints predominate, it cannot be compared for its harmonious beauty, to any other family chapel in Rome.

The rebuilding of the façade of S. Maria Maggiore is by Ferdinando Fuga. It is justly considered the masterpiece of that artist and has the merit of having preserved the precious mosaic that records the " miracle of the snow." In fact, the building of this Basilica is linked to a curious legend.

St. John Lateran

108

In the night of the 5th August 352 Pope Liberius and a patrician called John had a vision of the Madonna who told them to build a basilica on the spot where a heavy fall of snow would appear the following day, although it was the height of summer. On the dollowing day the Esquiline was covered with a blanket of snow which exactly followed the lines of the basilica to be built. Even though history tells us that it was Sixtus III and not Liberius (although the church is still called the Liberian Basilica), under whom the church was built, the Romans are very fond of this poetic origin. So, every year, at the beginning of August, a shower of white flowers is scattered from the cupola of the Pauline chapel on the altar where the miraculous image is vererated.

At the beginning of the Via Salaria one may see a typical example of eighteenth century architecture, Villa Albani built by Cardinal Alessandro Albani, nephew of Clement XI, approximately between 1746 and 1763, a work by Carlo Marchionni. The gardens are no longer laid out in rectangular beds, but in gracefully planned and various patterns. The taste for elegance was combined with the reborn love for Greek art. The villa was also the seat of a wonderful museum, which the cardinal, under the guidance of the German archaelogist, John James Winckelmann, used as the collection of all that remained of the most beautiful and precious of Graeco-Roman antiquity. Winckelmann was the great theorist of Neo-Classicism, known as the " father of archaeology ", who said that the only way to become great and, if possible, inimitable, was to imitate the ancients. Unfortunately the collection was rifled by Napoleon and the Albani sold many of the statues when they were given back, as they were in financial difficulties. At the present time, together with the remains of the Albani collection, the Villa houses some important collections of the Torlonia family, who are the present owners.

There are important sculptures by Canova in the National Museum of Modern Art, such as the colossal group of Hercules

S. Maria Maggiore

and Lyca, while, in the Villa Borghese, there is the famous " Conquering Venus," the sister of Napoloeon, Pauline Borghese, wife of Prince Camillo Borghese, carved half-naked on a bed, holding the apple of love victorious.

As we are in the Villa Borghese, we may proceed to the Pincio where, as we have said, there is the most significant monument of Neo-Classical Rome, together with the underlying Piazza del Popolo. Giuseppe Valadier, designer of this complex, had the same idea for the piazza as Bernini for Piazza S. Pietro, a circular piazza round an obelisk. The prospect of the Pincio, then occupied by gardens and precipices, was realised by using a superb natural background. In this way a true terrace was built; it is now famous owing to the that the best panorama of Rome is to be had from here.

Our itinerary through eighteenth century and Neo-Classical Rome goes from Piazza del Popolo through the picturesque Via del Babuino to Piazza di Spagna, with a deviation through Via di Ripetta, near which is Via Canova where the great master of Neo-Classic sculpture, Antonio Canova, had his studio. The house, red with fragments of ancient work let into the walls, is the inscription, « Sculpture issued reborn from this studio, through the work of Antonio Canova». Still near Piazza Augusto Imperatore, at the end of Via Ripetta, is the church of S. Rocco, with a façade by Valadier, after a work by the great Vicenza architect Andrea Palladio of the sixteenth century. The church was built at the beginning of the sixteenth century by the innkeepers and boatmen of Ripetta. When a port was built here two centuries later, by Clement XI, the church faced on the most important wharf for goods from Sabina and Umbria. The Porto di Ripetta (from the diminutive of " ripa ", bank) was designed by Alessandro Specchi and Carlo Fontana, using the travertine from one of the Colosseum arches which collapsed during the earthquake of 1703. The port was afterwards demolished to build the present Ponte Cavour. On the site the ancient

PIAZZA DEL POPOLO

marble hydrometer with the levels and dates of Tiber floods can still be seen.

The "Porto di Ripetta" was given this name to distinguish it from the port called "Ripa Grande" which had been rebuilt by Innocent XII for mooring the sailing vessels which came up the Tiber from the sea at Fiumicino. The depth of the river in those times was such that even the naval ships could tie up there. The chronicler Magalotti reports that on July 17th, 1683 the vice-roy of Naples « wishing to provide an entertainment for the city of Rome sent a fine galley with the poop and prow gilded to "Ripa Grande" ». Even after 1870 some torpedo boats have moored there. Up until the great walls of the Tiber were built brigantines could be seen tied up to the wharf with robust hawsers, for the most part loaded with Sicilian products, especially wines. The Romans used to go on board to drink a good glass of marsala or malvasia.

After this deviation, we come to Piazza di Spagna, a typical eighteenth century monument being provided by the animated monumental staircase which leads up from the Barcaccia Fountain to the church of Trinità dei Monti. It was built by Francesco de Sanctis with the bequest of a French diplomat under the reigns of Innocent XIII Conti and Benedict XIII Orsini. The artists' models of the Via Margutta studios, dressed in the costume of the Ciociaria, used to sell violets on the 137 steps of the theatrical Rococo staircase, adorned with flowers of every season. Even today, the fashion houses use the steps as a background to photograph their mannequins.

In nearby Via Condotti, the most chic street in Rome, which gets its name from the conduits of the Acqua Vergine which pass beneath it on the way to the Fontana dei Trevi, it is worth remembering the Caffè Greco, opened about 1760 by the Greek Nicola da Maddalena, an experienced coffee dealer, whose blends made his *caffè* the Mecca of intellectual life. Among his first and most illustrious custom-

TRINITA' DEI MONTI

114

ers was Goethe, lover of Rome, who finished the scenes of " Iphigenia in Tauris " there. At the end of the XVIII and beginning of the XIX centuries, the café became even more famous. Its most important clients were Chopin, Bizet, Berlioz, Rossini, Listz, Thorvaldsen, Wagner, d'Azeglio, Ibsen, Gogol and then Carducci, Sgambati and the Roman Pascarella.

Later on, Lord Tennyson, the poet and the English painter Joseph Severn, intimate friend of Keats, one of the greatest English poets of the early nineteenth century, lodged opposite the Café Greco. In the same house lived another English writer, William Makepeace Thackeray and it was there he wrote his famous " Prince Balbo " which was performed at the Barberini Theatre. Winkelmann also stayed in Via Condotti at the Locanda della Carrozza. For some time Stendhal stayed at no. 48, and at no. 81, Giacomo Leopardi.

Passing into Via del Corso, where there are numerous XVIII century monuments, especially in the side streets. Ve recall that from the end of the XVIII and for the first half of the XIX centuries it was the scene of the most gorgeous and gay Roman carnivals. The Corso, decorated with multicolured damasks hanging from windows and balconies of princely palaces, made a splendid picture. From the windows contests and challenges with the people below, with confetti and paper streamers took place. All this gaiety struck even Goethe who wrote, " At Rome, the Carnival is not a festival given to the people, but one which the people gives itself. The government makes no preparations and spends nothing and strangers act on their own account ... A simple signal authorises one to be mad and extravagant to one's heart's content and that, except for fighting with clubs and knives, everything is allowed; all classes intermingle and no-one takes offence for any damage suffered."

The signal which Goethe speaks of was the tolling of the Capitol bell, which gave the signal for the beginning and end

Trevi Fountain

of the Carnival, which lasted eight days. At the first stroke the carnival of men and animals began. There was a race, from Piazza del Popolo to Piazza Venezia, along the Corso, which had been cleared, of *Barberi*, wild, riderless horses, goaded in the flanks. The competition was dangerous to life and limb, and was forbidden at the time of King Umberto, after there had been an accident under the Royal balcony of Piazza Fiano, with Queen Margherita watching.

Returning to the monuments, there is, near the Pantheon, the Church of the Maddalena, a modest XIV century monument rebuilt by Carlo Fontana in the seventeenth. The concave façade, which was added in 1735 to the design of Giuseppe Sardi, with its statues and niches and the gorgeous organ inside, contribute to making it the most singular of Rococo churches. A short distance away, still to the right of the Corso going towards Piazza Venezia, is Piazza S. Ignazio, a jewel of XVIII century architecture. The movement of the little curvilinear palazzi shows genius. It is by the Beneventian architect Filippo Raguzzini, who was a favourite of Bendict XIII. The Via del Burrò leads out of this. The name " Burrò " comes from " bureaux ", as the French occupation offices at the beginning of the XIX century, were in this street, and also from the shape of the buildings.

Recrossing the Corso and entering the alley-ways on the other side, we reach the Piazza di Trevi, one of the most picturesque and famous piazzas of Rome. It owes its name to the water which issues from the famous fountain, that takes up the whole frontage of the palace of the Dukes of Poli. It is held to be typically eighteenth century for its rocks, gorgeousness, and the period of its building (from 1732 to 1762), but the spirit and form are of Bernini. It has been said that it forms the fabulous epilogue of Roman Baroque. It appears that the Roman architect Nicola Salvi carried out the work using a lost design of Bernini's. Indeed, if you ask a Roman for the name of its architect, he will probably give the name of Bernini, unconsciously giving an artistic appreciation that the critics have arrived at after long and painful research. It is enough to remember that the Fontana dei Trevi has been defined as a " plagiarism unparalleled in the history of art " and that it is " a seventeenth century work carried out in the eighteenth. Against this authoritative criticism must be set the opinion of the Roman who love and admire the fountain for its grandeur and beauty, rightly considering it the Queen of Fountains. It is certainly the most monumental in Rome. It was ordered by Clement XII as the superb *mostra* for the water known as Acqua Vergine or Trevi. These two names, commonly used for the water brought into Rome by Agrippa (son-in-law and collaborator of Augustus) in 19 B. C., originate as follows. The springs were found twelve kilometres from Rome in a zone known as " *Trebium* ", or three-cross-way, hence Trevi. The spring has three mounths, and also for this reason could have been called " Trevi ". It is said that the water was shown to some thirsty Roman soldiers by a girl (*virgo*), hence the name " Acqua Vergine ".

The belief that one may ensure one's return to Rome by throwing a coin in the fountain (over one's shoulder, however), is universally known. Less well known is an episode proved by a strange element in the fountain itself, which records a disagreement between Nicola Salvi, while he was building the fountain, and a barber (who was also according to the custom of the time, an apothecary), who had his shop on the right-hand side of the piazza in the red palace of the Castellani.

It seems that the chemist, or barber, as you will, at the end of his patience owing to the disorder reigning in the piazza, where enormous masses of travertine were piled, criticised the work of the artist and complained to his customers that they were obliged to see the reflection of the " ugly thing " in his mirror. Irritated by the barber's behaviour Nicola Salvi had a huge slab of marble put up on the right hand side of the baluster surrounding the fountain. On

PALACE OF THE CONSULTA

this he put a large amphora, which has no fellow on the other side. In this way, the barber's view was completely blocked, and all he could see in his mirror was the big vase, which according to the malicious intention of the artist, represented a barbers' lather-bowl.

The arteficers of the magnificent sculpture of the fountain were Gian Battista Maini who executed the central group with Neptune in a shell form chariot with rampant tritons and horses; Pietro Bracci, to whom we owe the group called the " Cavallo agitato ", (the restive horse) which symbolizes the restless aspects of the waters of the sea and also the contrasting " Cavallo placido ", (the placid horse); and Giuseppe Pannini who designed the two statues of " Abundance " and " Healthiness of the air ".

Worth mentioning in the last stretch of the Corso, near Piazza Venezia, are the palaces of Alessandro Specchi, now the Bank of Rome, and that of Doria, whose façade is by Gabriele Valvassori, sober and is harmonious even in its delicate caprices.

In Piazza Venezia we must make other deviations to follow our Roman eighteenth century and Neo-Classical itinerary, one towards Piazza SS. Apostoli and the Quirinal, one towards the Capitol and a third to St Peter's, going along Corso Vittorio Emanuele to Trastevere.

Piazza dei SS. Apostoli is dominated by the church of the same name, which dates from the VIth century, but is a Neo-Classical monument for the façade by Valadier and L. Righini and the sculptures of Canova which are inside. We refer to the monument to the engraver Giovanni Volpato, friend and patron of Canova, a bas-relief representing Friendship as a youth weeping over the tomb of his friend, and the mausoleum of Clement XIV (Frà Lorenzo Ganganelli), in which the artist revealed his genius by writing the first page of Neo-Classicism.

Going up through Via della Dataria to the Quirinal, we come to the Palazzo della Consulta, by Ferdinando Fuga,

S. Maria del Priorato on the Aventine

notable for decorative effect and the harmony of the ensemble. It was built by Clement XII for the Sacra Consulta, one of the most important of the Roman congregations.

In the architecture of this period it is impossible to ignore that of one of the most picturesque zones in the city, linked to the name of Rome's greatest illustrator during the XVIII century, the engraver, Giambattista Piranesi.

For the Grand Prior, Giovan Battista Rezzonico, after-wards Cardinal, Piranesi renewed the church of S. Maria del Priorato, of the Knights of Malta, on the Aventine, and closed the tranquil piazza overlooked by the Villa of the Knights, in fantastic architecture.

And so we arrive at the final stage of our itinerary, which takes us, after a short stretch of Corso Vittorio, to the *Teatro Argentina* (in the Largo of the same name) inaugurated in 1732 under the Pontificate of Clement XII and built to a design by the architect Marchese Girolamo Theodoli, who made of it a model of elegance and acoustics.

There are many memories linked to this theatre. We will confine ourselves to the fiasco of the " Barber of Seville ", on the 21st February 1816, owing, apart from a number of malicious enemies of Rossini's in audience, who were the supporters of Paisiello who had set the same libretto to music, to a series of unfortunate accidents. After the tenor had spent a long time tuning the guitar to serenade Rosina, one of the strings broke as soon as he began to sing, amid general laughter. Don Basilio came on stage, tripped over a brace and finished flat out in the auditorium. To crown all, a black cat came on to the stage and began careering round and round like a made thing. The hubbub was so great that the curtain had to be rung down. Rossini, who was in the house for the first night, left the theatre. But the Romans wished to make up for this unfortunate evening by demonstrating under the windows of his house in Via dei Leutari the following evening, thence carrying him in triumph to the Argentina, where the notes of the "Barber" had earned just recognition and a great success.

On the left, proceeding along the Corso Vittorio, near Piazza Farnese, is the little church of S. Maria della Quercia, with a convex façade by Filippo Raguzzini, already mentioned as the author of the suggestive Piazza S. Ignazio. He may be considered as the most representative of the Roman builders of the eighteenth century who drew inspiration from French Rococo.

Sill in Corso Vittorio Emanuele is Palazzo Braschi by Cosimo Morelli (1790 and following years), the last of the palaces of papal families (that of Pius VI, 1775-1779), a typical example of Neo-Renaissance architecture, to be remembered especially for the Scalone, (great Staircase), one of the finest in Rome, and for the statue of "Pasquino", the torso of a Hellenistic statue, which is attached to it, famous for the "Pasquinades", biting satires which were attached to the statue from the sixteenth century on.

The "pasquinate" often took the form of vivacious dialogue with other typical personages among the stone statues of ancient or medieval Rome such as Marforio, Madame Lucrezia, Abate Luigi and the Facchino. The name probably comes from that of a witty hunchbacked tailor who had a workshop here in the XVth century and seems to have been the originator of the genre.

Since 1952 the Braschi Palace has been the seat of the Museum of Rome which has a specialized collection of documents relative to Roman topography and to the usages and customs of the city from the middle ages down to the present day.

Even in the Vatican and St Peter's there are notable Neo-Classical monuments. We mention the Pio-Clementine museum, built by order of Clement XIV and Pius VI, and works by Canova in the Basilican the stele of the Stuarts and Clement XIII's mausoleum, one of his most successful works. An amusing episode is linked to this monument.

At the feet of the Pontiff, who is in an attitude of prayer, there are two lions, representing the strength of Pope Rezzonico. Among the collaborators of Canova there was a sculptor whose surname was Elephant. He asked on several occasions that his name be inscribed on the monument. He was satisfied in a very odd way : the artist carved the tail of the lions in such a way that when one looks at his hindquarters, the tail looks like an elephant's trunk. This detail, which may be noted by looking carefully at the lion in question, shows that the modest aspiration of Canova's assistant was met in a most original way.

Our journey across eighteenth century and Neo-Classical Rome finishes in Trastevere, in Via della Lungara, in front of Palazzo Corsini. The building dates from the time of Cardinal Domenico Riario, nephew of Sixtus IV, but its actual form was given it by Ferdinando Fuga. The cultured and eccentric Queen Christina, who transferred herself to Rome after embracing the Catholic faith and having abdicated, lived and died in this Palace.

In this palace, the Queen united that group of men of letters who afterwards founded the Academy known as " Arcadia ". Joseph Bonaparte lived there also, in 1797, as ambassador of the Directoire, and General Duphot, fiancé of Pauline Bonaparte, afterwards Pauline Borghese. He was killed in a riot between the Palace and the nearby Porta Settimiana. At the moment the palace is the headquarters of the National Academy of the Lincei.

CHAPTER VI

MODERN AND CONTEMPORARY ROME

WITHIN THE LIMITS set by our itinerary, it is not easy to follow the development of Rome since 1870, which is linked to a long period dense with history and the radical changes brought about by such inventions and discoveries as the telephone, the internal combustion engine, radio, television and the use of atomic energy. Papal Rome had 200,000 inhabitants, modern Rome 2,000,000. It extends in all directions beyond the ancient Aurelian Wall. With an impressive rhythm, broken only by two wars, after which there was an even more intense recovery, Rome since 1870 has become not only a capital city, but a Metropolis.

We shall try to follow this expansion as far as possible in our itinerary, which must obviously be sketchy, as it comprises the whole area of the city, that is, more than 579 square miles.

The first thrust of the city after 1870 was towards Porta Pia. Via Nazionale was straightened, Stazione Termini and Quintino Sella promoted the building of the first Ministries (the Finance Ministry), and the first steps were taken towards developing in the direction of Monte Sacro.

At about the same time, Rome spread across the Tiber, where a new district develiped, that of Prati, afterwards dominates by the monumental Palace of Justice. Great new buildings for the new necessities of Rome rose one after the other, and the expansion considerably exceeded the de-

125

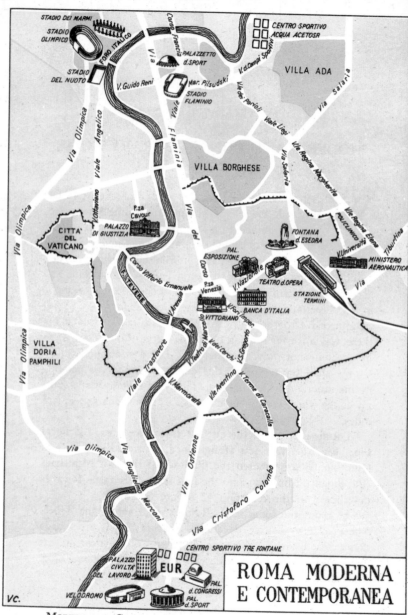

MODERN AND CONTEMPORARY ROME

mand. In fact, it had been prophesied that the population would reach 2,000,000 in twenty years. Instead, it merely doubled, by the beginning of this century, and a crisis in the building trade arose such as had never been known in Italy.

At the end of the nineteenth century and the beginning of the twentieth, monumental complexes such as that to Victor Emmanuel II, the Palace of Exhibitions, the Banca d'Italia building in Via Nazionale, the Policlinico, which, together with the wonderful Passegiata Archeologica, we owe to Guido Baccelli, with the embankments of the Tiber which had so often flooded and caused damage, were built.

After World War I, the city went on growing in every direction, Monteverde, Monte Mario, Parioli, Monte Sacro, Ostiense, Tiburtino, end the centre of Rome was completely changed by fascist clearance and rebuilding schemes, which gave rise to the Via dei Fori Imperiali, Via S. Gregorio, and Via del Teatro di Marcello, isolating and improving the position of the most important ancient monuments. The Città Universitaria (University) was built and the foundations laid for the expansion of the city towards the sea with the creation of the so-called E.42 zone (E.U.R.), intended for an international exhibition prevented by the outbreak of World War II.

In the second post-war period the city quickly reached the 2,000,000 inhabitants wrongly predicted for 1900. This increase has provoked a fresh building boon, which is often disordered, giving rise to suburbs, owing to the political and religious importance of Rome as the centre of Roman Catholicism (*Caput Mundi*), which is becoming, as we have said, a Metropolis. The great, new railway station and the international airport at Fiumicino help to give the impression that Rome is the centre of the world.

The 1960 Olympics' an event of exceptional world importance have helped to give Rome an up-to-date complex of sports centres and stadiums. Rome in the Olympic year has a character all its own, with buildings which are both functional and monumental, much admired by all nations for the grandeur and daring of their lines.

This short summary of development in the last ninety years gives an idea of the extent of the subject which we must deal with in a some idea of the material to be dealt with in a short space. As far as we can follow chronologically we shall begin with Via Nazionale.

Mgr. Francis Xavier de Merode, pro-minister of weapons under Pius IX, a wealthy Belgian prelate, was the instigator of Via Nazionale with a plan to extend the city towards the Castro Pretorio zone, where the Stazione Termini is now. An agreement was signed in 1867 with the Roman Senate, for the selling off of land at ridiculously low prices as building lots. The stretch of Via Nuova Pia (now Via Nazionale) was traced from the Quattro Fontane crossroads to Via delle Terme at the same time as Stazione Termini was started. The road, built with modern ideas through gardens and vineyards, was lined with persimmon trees. No one knew that the fuit was eatable.

This brought development outside the limits of Old Rome, and the Palace of Exhibitions and the Opera were built, as well as the splendid Naiad Fountain.

The Palace of Exhibitions was built to the design of Pio Piacentini in 1882. The Opera, in Via Firenze, off Via Nazionale was built in 1880 by Costanzi, owner of the Quirinale Hotel (architect Achille Sfondrini) and inaugurated with the " Semiramide " of Gioacchino Rossini on 20th November 1880. It was bought by the state and restored in 1926 by Marcello Piacentini, who also modernised it, only a few months before his recent death.

The Naiads' Fountain dates originally fron ten days before the entry of the National Army through Porta Pia in 1870. It was intended by Pius IX to be a plain basin at ground level, surrounded by jets, as the " mostra " of the Acqua Marcia. He had had this water brought again to Rome by Moraldi, under the name of Acqua Pia. It was inaugurated

7. S. MARIA IN COSMEDIN

8. PALAZZO OF SPORT

on 10th September 1870, on the site now occupied by the monument to the Fallen of Dogali, and Pius IX is said to have joked on the name of Marcia, now Pia (Pious). In 1885, when the Piazza dell'Esedra was re-planned, it was decided to transfer the fountain there. The design is by Alessandro but the 1900 decorations are by Mario Rutelli.

There were many fierce discussions about the " shameless Naiads " as they were seen through the hoardings, at the City Council. One night in February 1901, students demolished the hoarding, and no-one dared to oppose this *de facto*. The central group, with the vigorous god grappling with the great fish — " man conquering the brute force of nature " — was added in 1910.

The four female statues represent the nymphs of the rivers, lakes, seas and underground waters. The fountain has a beautiful effect at night when it is lit, and gives an excellent first impression of Rome to anyone arriving at Stazione Termini. This Station, universally admired both for its beauty and utility, was built in 1950, to replace the old station of the last years of Papal Rome, with its population of 200,000. Many reconstructions were rendered necessary by the new necessities of the Italian capital and in 1938 it was decided to rebuild it. Work was interrupted by the was, and it was completed ten years ago.

There are two modern monuments behind the station, the University and the Policlinico. The latter was built by the Roman Giulio Podesti, between 1888 and 1898 by the great doctor, Guido Baccelli. The University took the place of the old Sapienza, now out of date, and was built in 1935 by Marcello Piacentini. At hand is the Air Ministry, also modern, near the Campo Verano, the cemetery of Rome, started under Gregory XVI in 1837.

Near Viale Regina, which was also opened after Rome became capital, there is another district interesting architecturally, by the architect Gino Coppedè, a skilful Florentine artist, in 1926. He was a clever wood carver and brought this ability to his architecture, creating this little district which takes his name for the richness of the carving, which make it striking. Note the plaque to Gigli on the gate of the Villa where he lived in Via Serchio.

From the Policlinico and the University to Via Labicana and the Colosseum, one passes to Via dei Fori Imperiali and Via Gregoriana, which we have already mentioned, and which date from 1932.

At Piazza Venezia, we have the Memorial to Victor Emmanuel II, inaugurated in 1911 for the Golden Jubilee of the Proclamation of the Kingdom, in honour of the Father of the Fatherland, who had achieved Italian Unity. The monument, debatable today because it clashes with its surroundings, is the largest of the New Italy. It was built by the Marchisan architect Giuseppe Sacconi and is a monumental staircase rising between three tree-grown half-circles, added later, to the Altar of the Fatherland, with the harmonious architectural and sculptural composition of the Statue Of Rome, in the middle, by Angelo Zanelli. The Tomb of the Unknown Warrior was put at the foot of this in 1921.

The Corso Vittorio Emanuele, which is gained through Via del Plebiscito from Piazza Venezia was built in 1886, using part of the ancient Via Papale, along which the Popes would pass from S. John Lateran to St Peters'. It forms the true entrance to the Borghi and St Peter's over the Vittorio Emanuele bridge. Via Arenula and Ponte Garibaldi are the main entrance to Trastevere, the old popular quarter, rich in tradition and crowded restaurants, where even today the " Festa de Noantri " takes place (" Our Own Feast ").

There is a procession in honour of Madonna del Carmine on the 16th of July every year. Competitions of amateur poets and the presentation of new Roman songs, amuse the visitor in the streets and the brightly lit piazzas of the quarter. The feast of S. Giovanni, celebrated in the St John Lateran zone every year on the night of the 23 June, dedicated to life and gaiety, is also dear to the Roman heart. It was once

Altar of the Fatherland

the feast of Ceres, the corn goddess, to obtain a good harvest. At the beginning of this century, people gathered on the occasion of this feast to see the ceremonious return from the Capannelle racecourse, with the King driving his own royal carriage usually preceded by that of the Queen with bewigged and red-liveried footmen.

Returning from S. Giovanni, to which the traditional festivals have brought us, we return to the other side of the Tiber, where we find another large building, the Palace of Justice. The zone which began with its building — it took from 1880 to 1910 — was in those days the last word in " modernity ". It, like Via Nazionale, is owed to Mgr Francis Xavier de Merode, who bought up a number of farms and vineyards along the Tiber and thus began the building of private houses. The zone developed very quickly after the City Council had built barracks and a parade ground there, particularly after the building of Ponte Margherita in 1891 and Ponte Cavour in 1901, at the point where the old ferry raft of the famous riverman Toto Bigi, known as " ferrobotte " used to operate.

The Palace of Justice is by Guglielmo Calderini. He took his inspiration from the grandiose buildings of the XVII century, and wanted it even bigger than it is, certain technicians advanced the theory that the bank of the Tiber at that point would not carry the weight (they were wrong). However, the Ministry of Public Works relieved Calderini of the task and he died of grief.

The meadows of the Castello, that great expanse of green in the midst of which Castel S. Angelo rose, soon became a vast, widestreeted residential quarter. It was noted by some (rightly) that anti-clericalism prevented any of the streets from being directed towards the splendid view of the dome of St Peter's, but one has to admit that, with its wide streets and piazzas, it is better able to deal with modern traffic than many zones built in recent times.

The birth of Olympic Rome is linked to the 1960 games. It has a special topography and aspect that deserves an itinerary apart, as it is not confined to one area, but is scattered in various parts of the city, although it has a unity of aspect due not only to the exterior aspect but to utility.

Its heart is the Foro Italico (ex Mussolini), connected with three other areas, that is, the EUR, the new zone through which the Via Cristoforo Colombo runs, and destined for future development under the town-planning scheme, the wide area between Via Flaminia and Ponte Flaminio, dominated by the hill of Villa Glori, and Acqua Acetosa.

The Foro Italico was designed by the architects Enrico Del Debbio and Luigi Moretti and built in 1932. The Olympic Stadium was built immediately after the war (also called Stadium of the hundred thousand because it holds that number of people) and the swimming pool was finished in 1959, an oasis of freshness in the city, destined both for the general public and for swimmers. It has every size of pool and has every modern technical and sporting convenience.

The Olympic Road passes from the Trionfale quarter through the Lungotevere Cadorna, the Circonvallazione Clodia, Circonvallazione Trionfale, Via Angelo Emo, over the Magliana bridge and on to the Via Cristoforo Colombo to the EUR, the zone now known by these initials (Esposizione Universale di Roma), since, had it not been for the war, there would have been an international exhibition there in 1942. A residential quarter has already arisen around the monumental buildings intended for the exhibition and now destined partly as offices and partly as museums and Government Records Offices. Noteworthy are the Palace of Italian Civilisation (the " Square Colosseum "), the church of SS Peter and Paul, and the Palace of Congresses, with the bold Nervi ceiling.

The zone is reached by the wide Via Cristoforo Colombo which connects Rome with the sea, is the quickest way to Naples and is particularly suited for a sports centre.

200 yards from the piazza containing a stele to Marconi, carved by the sculptor Arturo Dazzi, rises the Palace of Sport, a gigantic building in cylindrical form, more than 300 yards round the base and a hundred feet high, by the architects Pier Luigi Nervi and Marcello Piacentini. It is surrounded by a glass wall 65 feet high which leghts a gallery designed ti lead to the steps of the huge arena and to be a placefor exhibitions of all kinds. It is thirty yards wide and serves as a promenade between one sporting event and another. The arena has a diameter of 50 yards and serves for boxing, basketball, tennis, fencing, hockey on roller-skates and gymnastic events.

There are three great artificial lakes fed by a great artificial waterfall at the foot of the hill on which it stands. The first is at the foot of the Palace, while the other two are bounded by the Via Cristoforo Colombo, which is two-way at this point, one branch leading to Naples and the sea and the other to Rome.

Near by, the Rose Swimming Pool is already open to the public. It takes its name from the dominating adornment. In the same EUR zone there is a Velodrome for cycle racing with a quarter-mile track and a stand for 20,000 spectators. Lastly, on either side of the Via Cristoforo Colombo there are 25 acres of ground given over to a sports centre comprising grounds for Soccer, Rugby, hockey, Skating, tracks and gymnasia. Very up-to-date, this is destined to the younger generation.

Starting again from the Foro Italico, crossing the river over the Ponte Duca d'Aosta, we arrive on the Flaminia where there is the Olympic Village for the accomodation of competitors, the Palazzetto dello Sport and the new Stadio Flaminio.

The Olympic Village, like other buildings put up for this occasion, is designed both to house Olympic athletes and to serve the citizenry, it will become a residential quarter within the Town-Planning scheme after the Olympics. The new district, which stretches between the Tiber and the green hill of Villa Glori with the Remembrance Park, can accomodate 8,000 people. It is not a specialised zone for athletes, but can easily be changed into a living area. The architecture is of residential type and the rooms have large windows, sometimes occupying the whole wall.

There are other important sports centres in this zone, the Palazzetto dello Sport and the Stadio Flaminio.

The former is at the end of the monumental Ponte Flaminio, linking Rome to the Via Cassia and Via Flaminia. The building, a new departure in architecture, is the work of the architects Nervi and Vitellozzi. It is in ferro-concrete and is circular, with a spherical cupola having a light of some 85 yards and has a competition hall inside of 17 yards diameter. It is 50 feet high. It holds 6000 and can be used for tennis, basketball, skating, fencing, boxing, wrestling and weight-lifting. It is air-conditioned and can be lit with sun-lamps at night.

A short way off is the rebuilt Stadio Nazionale which has been rechristened Stadio Flaminio. The new building which occupies the area of the old can accomodate more people. This is produced by a leap up in the terracing by the architect, Nervi, who has a justly earned world reputation for work in ferro-concrete.

To complete the picture of Olympic Rome it is enough to go to Acqua Acetosa, beyond the hill of Parioli where another grandiose sports centre has been completed over an area of 200,000 square yards, giung to the foot of Monte Antenne, ince part of Villa Savoia. There will be a complex of buildings and an up-to-date athletic medical centre, to which the University Faculty for this branch of Medicine will transfer.

A number of famous architects have worked for this wonderful complex. We mention, among those already named, the planners of the Olympic Village, Vittorio Cafiero, Adalberto Libera, Amedeo Luccichenti, Vincenzo Monaco and Luigi Moretti. So a new type of architecture, giving life to a new Rome, has been born, which will remain into the future to testify to this 1960, linked to a meeting going back to ancient Greece and on which the eyes of the world will be focussed.

INDEX

ALPHABETICAL INDEX

Confined to those subjects which the author has treated at length

TABLE OF CONTENTS

A small plan of the monuments is printed at the beginning of each chapter.

INDEX OF ILLUSTRATIONS

PLATES

PRINTED IN JULY, 1960 IN THE WORKS OF THE SOC. A.B E.T.E.
VIA PRENESTINA, 683 - ROME